Inverse Paranoid

Turning Challenges into Opportunities

RAJA KUMAR

Foreword by **Umesh Madhyan**
Chief Operating Officer, Leap India
Former VP-Logistics, Hindustan Coca-Cola Beverages

INDIA • SINGAPORE • MALAYSIA

ISBN
Paperback 979-8-89699-764-1
Hardcase 979-8-89744-693-3

Appreciation for Inverse Paranoid

1. "Inverse Paranoid" stands out with its unique philosophy of reframing struggles as blessings. Raja Kumar's storytelling and practical tools make this book both relatable and transformative. It's a beacon of hope for anyone stuck in life's rut. **Nitin Gupta, Director - Aircraft Financing, IndiGo Airlines**

2. "Inverse Paranoid" by Raja Kumar challenges readers to see life's adversities as opportunities, offering a transformative mindset rooted in resilience and gratitude. With authenticity and actionable insights, Raja inspires us to embrace the belief that life always works for our growth and success.

   Ashish Mendiratta, Former Director Supply Chain - Asia Pacific, Kohler Co., Former Supply Chain Director, Philips Electronics India Ltd

3. Raja Kumar's authenticity shines in "Inverse Paranoid." His philosophy of reframing adversity as a gift is life-changing. With relatable examples and practical tools, this book is a treasure for personal and professional growth.

   Mohit Sawhney, VP, Macquarie Global Pvt Ltd

4. "In today's fast-paced world, where demands on our time and energy seem to multiply daily, finding moments of clarity and effective solutions to life's everyday challenges can feel like a

Herculean task. Raja has beautifully put together a concise guide to navigating the complexities of professional & personal life. It cuts through the noise and delivers practical, actionable advice that you can implement immediately. No complex jargon or theoretical frameworks here – just clear, relatable insights that resonate with the realities of the modern times."

Shammi Dua, VP-A.T. Kearney

5. Packed with wisdom and authenticity, this book teaches you how to turn setbacks into stepping stones. Raja Kumar's life lessons resonate deeply, making "Inverse Paranoid" an empowering read for those seeking purpose and success.

Ranjeet Jha, VP-Technology, Policybazaar

6. "This book presents a transformative perspective, encouraging readers to view life as working in their favor rather than against them. Raja Kumar's practical insights, drawn from personal experiences, simplify complex ideas, making them accessible and relatable. An inspiring read for anyone looking to reshape their narrative and achieve success."

Pankaj Bansal, General Manager, National High Speed Rail Corporation Ltd

7. Raja Kumar's Inverse paranoid is a life guide to harmonious living, to unlock secrets towards productive and healthy living and finding solutions in everyday life. It helps us overcoming obstacles with ease. A must read.

Sanjay Lazar, Bestselling author of "ON ANGELS WINGS", Former Team Lead, Air India Limited

Contents

Section 1: Foundations of a Balanced Life

Section 2: Mastering Productivity and Personal Growth

Section 3: Wisdom and Resilience in Adversity

Section 4: Life Lessons and Timeless Truths

Reader Profile

This book is for dreamers, doers, and those caught somewhere in between—people who strive for success but face challenges that sometimes feel insurmountable. If you've ever felt stuck in the rut of procrastination, battled self-doubt, or struggled to align your actions with your goals, this book is your guide. Whether you're a student looking for direction, a professional juggling responsibilities, or someone simply seeking a more meaningful life, the lessons shared here will resonate with you.

It's for anyone who wants to turn struggles into stepping stones, embrace resilience, and unlock their full potential. You don't need a perfect start; you just need a willingness to learn and a belief that the best is yet to come.

About the Author

Mr. Raja Kumar is a serial star performer of India's Number 1 Passenger Car Company. Currently serving as Department Head - Export Warehouse at his organisation, he boasts a remarkable list of accomplishments, including the prestigious Under 40 Supply Chain Super Achiever award and four recognitions from the Managing Director of his current organisation.

His contributions extend beyond the workplace. He has been commended by the Delhi Police Commissioner for his efforts in promoting road safety. With a social media following of over 50,000, Raja Kumar guides young professionals and students on LinkedIn.

His first book "Elite Performer: How to be Exceptional at Work" was widely appreciated by young professionals.

Through "Inverse Paranoid", Raja Kumar shares the strategies and insights that have fueled his professional success. Whether for newcomers or seasoned professionals, the book offers valuable guidance to help individuals unlock their full potential and excel in their careers. All these lessons and experiences are compiled in "Inverse Paranoid".

You can contact him at:

Website: www.motivationdrive.com

Email: rajakumar13oct@gmail.com

Preface

In a world that often amplifies negativity and encourages a mindset of scarcity, adopting a positive perspective is more than just wishful thinking—it's a transformative practice. *Inverse Paranoid* delves into a revolutionary way of thinking that shifts the focus from fear and doubt to faith and abundance. Inspired by the teachings of W. Clement Stone and deeply rooted in biblical principles, this book invites readers to reframe their experiences and embrace the belief that life's challenges are designed to enrich, empower, and advance them.

The philosophy of "Inverse Paranoid" invites us to believe that the universe conspires in our favor. Instead of succumbing to the mindset that the world is conspiring against us, we learn to trust that the world—and more importantly, God—is working for our good. Drawing from powerful scriptures and practical insights, this book demonstrates how our thoughts, beliefs, and words shape the reality we experience.

Through relatable examples and profound truths, the pages ahead will challenge you to guard your heart, renew your mind, and expect goodness in every aspect of your life. Whether you're facing economic downturns, personal trials, or societal pressures, this approach empowers you to rise above circumstances and thrive, regardless of external conditions.

This is more than just a philosophy—it's a call to action. To live as an inverse paranoid is to align with faith, hope, and divine promise. As you embark on this journey, may you discover the extraordinary power of seeing life through the lens of abundance, and may this book inspire a renewed sense of purpose and joy in your life.

Foreword

Life is a remarkable journey, shaped not only by the moments of triumph but also by the challenges that test our spirit and resolve. It is in these moments of uncertainty that we often discover our truest potential, and it is precisely this perspective that Raja Kumar's Inverse Paranoid offers to readers. This book is more than just a collection of ideas—it is a powerful guide to transforming how we perceive the world and our place within it.

I first came across Raja Kumar's story through his widely celebrated book Elite Performer: How to Be Exceptional at Work, and what struck me most was his ability to connect life's struggles with actionable insights for personal and professional growth. In Inverse Paranoid, Raja goes even deeper, presenting a philosophy that challenges us to look beyond adversity and embrace the belief that life is conspiring for our benefit, not against us.

The concept of being an "inverse paranoid" may seem radical in a world often dominated by negativity, but it is this very shift in mindset that makes the idea so powerful. Inspired by W. Clement Stone's teachings and grounded in biblical principles, this book compels us to reframe how we see challenges—not as setbacks, but as opportunities for growth, wisdom, and transformation. Raja has taken these timeless principles and made them accessible to anyone willing to take the courageous step of rethinking their perspective.

What makes this book stand out is Raja Kumar's authenticity. Drawing from his personal journey—from a humble upbringing in a 10x10 room to becoming a leader and mentor—he speaks from experience. His life is a testament to the power of resilience, gratitude, and a growth mindset. He doesn't just theorize about overcoming adversity; he has lived it. His story is proof that anyone, regardless of their starting point, can rise above their circumstances and create a life of purpose and abundance.

The lessons in this book are not just philosophical musings—they are practical tools for everyday life. Raja's insights into time management, resilience, and mental strength are rooted in real-world experiences. Whether you're a young professional navigating the complexities of your career or a seasoned leader seeking renewed purpose, the principles in Inverse Paranoid will resonate deeply.

As you turn these pages, you will encounter stories of courage and determination, along with strategies that challenge you to rethink how you approach life's difficulties. From embracing simplicity to conquering overthinking, this book offers a roadmap to unlock your full potential. More importantly, it inspires you to trust in the process of life, knowing that every challenge is a step toward something greater.

Raja Kumar's Inverse Paranoid is a gift to anyone ready to rewrite their story. It is a call to action—a reminder that the world, despite its hardships, holds immense beauty and opportunity for those willing to see it. As you embark on this journey, may you find not just inspiration but also the courage to embrace life with faith, hope, and a renewed sense of purpose.

– Umesh Madhyan

Chief Operating Officer, Leap India

Former VP-Logistics, Hindustan Coca-Cola Beverages

A Journey from Struggles to Success

Life is a series of trials, each shaping us into who we are meant to become. My story begins in a single room—10 feet by 10 feet—shared by my family of four and my grandmother. It wasn't just a house; it was a space filled with resilience, hope, and lessons that would form the foundation of my life's purpose. A single community water tap served 50 to 60 families in our colony, and a shared toilet meant waiting in line for over an hour. Yet, amidst these struggles, there was a quiet strength that kept us moving forward.

As I look back, these moments weren't just challenges—they were chapters in a story that taught me lessons more valuable than gold. Speaking of gold, I still remember the day when the last of our family's jewelry was sold to buy books for my 12th-grade studies. It was a moment of sacrifice, love, and determination that would forever drive me to strive for something greater.

One particular turning point stands out vividly. My mother worked as a house help, and the families she served often passed down their old clothes for me to wear. One day, someone looked at my worn-out shirt and casually assumed I too worked as a house help. That moment pierced my heart, not because of shame, but because of resolve. I promised myself that I would achieve something so significant that those same people would look at me in awe, not pity.

While facing these challenges, I learned about the truly important things in life: the value of time, the strength of resilience, and the power of mindset. I discovered that life's unbreakable rules—like setting boundaries, overcoming procrastination, and embracing simplicity—can serve as a compass, guiding us through the storms. I realized that thriving isn't about material possessions but about living with purpose, understanding life's harsh truths, and seizing the opportunities that come our way.

This journey also introduced me to the concept of being an *Inverse Paranoid*. Instead of believing that the world was conspiring against me, I began to view every challenge, every obstacle, and every hardship as an opportunity. I told myself that life wasn't happening *to* me—it was happening *for* me. Each setback wasn't a curse but a disguised blessing, nudging me closer to my goals. That shift in mindset changed everything. It allowed me to face difficulties with hope instead of despair, with action instead of hesitation. The stormy days of collecting rainwater in leaking buckets became symbols of resilience. The long waits for water or toilets became lessons in patience and gratitude.

This book is not just a reflection of my journey; it is a guide for anyone facing their own battles. Through these pages, you will explore strategies for conquering overthinking, achieving 10x improvement, and creating a morning routine that sets the tone for success. You'll uncover the wisdom of timeless concepts like SISU, the Finnish spirit of resilience, and Aristotle's Four Causes, which help us understand the "why" behind everything.

Every challenge I faced was a lesson in disguise, and every lesson became a stepping stone toward building a meaningful life. With the mindset of an *Inverse Paranoid*, I was able to see those challenges as gifts from the universe, designed to help me grow stronger, wiser, and more resilient.

Now, I invite you to walk this path with me, chapter by chapter, as we uncover the truths, strategies, and insights that can transform our lives. No matter where you start, remember this: the only limits are the ones you place on yourself. Let's begin.

Section 1

Foundations of a Balanced Life

When I was a child, our small house had a leaky roof that turned every rainy season into a battlefield. The walls, damp and discolored, bore witness to countless monsoons, and every year the story repeated itself. Buckets, pots, and pans became our frontline defense, strategically placed beneath the persistent drips from above. Each thunderstorm brought with it not just water but also a sense of urgency, as my family scrambled to minimize the damage. I can still hear the rhythmic ping of raindrops striking metal, a sound that felt both soothing and exasperating at once.

It was exhausting. My parents worked tirelessly to shield our home, and my brother and I would help in any way we could, moving the utensils around as new leaks appeared. Yet, amidst this chaos, something magical often happened. My grandmother, seated calmly amidst the scattered utensils, would smile and say, ***"True luxuries are not about the size of your home but the size of your heart."***

Her words, spoken with such conviction, were a beacon of light in those stormy times. She had lived through hardships far greater than a leaky roof, and her wisdom reminded us to look beyond the immediate discomfort. Despite our limited means, she found joy in the smallest pleasures—a warm meal, a good story, or the laughter of her grandchildren. Her perspective was a lesson in itself, teaching me that luxury wasn't about having more but appreciating what you already have.

As I grew older, the memory of those rainy days stayed with me, not as a reminder of struggle but as a testament to resilience and adaptability. I began to understand that life isn't about chasing extravagance or perfection but finding contentment in the simplest moments. Those days taught me how to adapt to circumstances and, more importantly, to embrace life's unbreakable rules. One of those rules is to cherish time, a treasure that slips away all too quickly.

Back then, I didn't realize how often we waste time on trivial pursuits. The rainstorms taught me to focus on what truly mattered—family, love, and shared effort. Each drop that fell into our buckets was a reminder of how fleeting life can be, and I learned to eliminate distractions that didn't serve my goals. Whether it was procrastinating on schoolwork or wasting hours on meaningless tasks, I began to see time as a resource too precious to squander.

It wasn't an easy lesson to learn. Growing up, I watched people around me struggle to strike a balance between work and family, between obligations and dreams. I realized that the choices we make between the ages of 20 and 55 often define the rest of our lives. This phase is a golden window to build a foundation for the future, yet many of us let it slip away by focusing on the wrong things.

My grandmother's quiet wisdom also instilled in me a sense of mortality. I also learned to cultivate mental strength. As I navigated the ups and downs of life, I realized that mentally strong people refuse to indulge in self-pity or waste energy on things they can't control. Instead, they focus on what they can change, just as my family did during those rainy seasons. The leaking roof didn't break us; it united us in our efforts and strengthened our resolve.

Looking back, those rainy days were more than just a period of hardship—they were a masterclass in resilience, adaptability, and perspective. They taught me to value the simple pleasures in life and to approach challenges with patience and grace. These lessons have stayed with me, influencing how I view time, manage my energy, and face life's inevitable difficulties.

The chapters in this section delve deeper into these truths. They explore the importance of embracing simplicity, managing time effectively, and adhering to life's unbreakable rules. They reveal the tough truths we must face to simplify our lives and the strategies mentally strong people use to overcome challenges. Together, they form a guide to living a harmonious, purpose-driven life, much like the one my grandmother envisioned amidst the raindrops.

Chapter 1

The True Luxuries of Life: Embracing Simple Pleasures

In our modern, fast-paced society, luxury is often associated with material wealth and lavish experiences. Yet, the essence of true luxury lies not in opulence, but in the simple, everyday pleasures that bring us genuine contentment and peace. Here's a look at some of the true luxuries in life that are often overlooked but offer profound satisfaction.

1. A Restful Sleep

One of life's greatest treasures is the ability to enjoy a restful night's sleep. In our modern age, where stress and responsibilities often lead to restless nights, the luxury of a full, uninterrupted sleep is invaluable. When we sleep soundly, our bodies and minds are able to rejuvenate, which contributes to overall well-being and clarity. The ability to retire for the night and wake up feeling refreshed and invigorated is a rare luxury in itself, one that enhances both our physical and mental health.

2. Relaxed Mornings

Another genuine luxury is the pleasure of relaxed mornings. Unlike the hectic pace of a typical day, starting the morning slowly provides a sense of peace and control. Without the stress of looming deadlines or the frantic scramble to leave the house, we can indulge in the simple joys of a quiet cup of coffee, a leisurely breakfast, or even a few moments of reflection. This unhurried start allows us to ease into the day, setting a positive and serene tone for the hours that follow. It's a chance to reconnect with ourselves, breathe deeply, and appreciate the tranquility of the early hours. Embracing these relaxed mornings transforms the start of the day into a small yet meaningful luxury, enriching our overall well-being and setting the stage for a more balanced and fulfilling day.

3. An Enjoyable Book

There is an unparalleled joy in losing oneself in the pages of a captivating book. Reading offers an escape into different worlds, perspectives, and stories, providing a unique form of relaxation and enrichment. Whether it's a gripping novel, an inspiring biography, or a thought-provoking essay, the luxury of reading allows us to explore new ideas and experiences from the comfort of our own space. This form of intellectual and emotional engagement is a true luxury that enriches our lives in countless ways.

4. Time for Fun

Amid the hectic pace of daily life, carving out time for enjoyment and relaxation can often seem like a rare luxury. However, the ability to indulge in activities that bring joy and playfulness is a true luxury. Whether it's spending time with loved ones, engaging in hobbies, or simply taking a break to enjoy a favorite pastime, the freedom to play and relax contributes to our overall happiness and well-being. Embracing these moments of lightheartedness allows us to reconnect with ourselves and the world around us.

5. Hearing Birds Chirping

One of life's most underrated luxuries is the chance to immerse yourself in the soothing sounds of nature, particularly the melodious songs of birds. Their gentle chirping offers a calming backdrop, turning even the most mundane moments into peaceful experiences. Pausing to listen to these natural harmonies can bring about a deep sense of tranquility and a closer connection to the natural world. This quiet pleasure serves as a reminder of the serenity and beauty that nature provides, a true luxury amidst the chaos of everyday life.

Words of Wisdom: The best pair in the world is smile and cry. They won't meet each other at a time; if they meet, that is the best moment in your life.

– Dr. A.P.J. Abdul Kalam

Chapter 2

Life's Unbreakable Rules: A Guide to Harmonious Living

Life is a journey filled with interactions, decisions, and relationships. Navigating this journey smoothly often requires adhering to certain timeless principles that foster positive relationships and personal growth. Here are five essential guidelines that can serve as your compass in leading a more fulfilling and harmonious life.

1. Steer Clear of Conflicts

Disagreements and disputes are inevitable, but they rarely lead to positive outcomes. Arguments often exacerbate tensions, damage relationships, and leave both parties dissatisfied. Instead of diving into a confrontation, seek to understand the other person's perspective. Approach differences with a mindset of finding common ground rather than proving a point. By avoiding unnecessary conflicts, you preserve your peace of mind and build stronger, more respectful relationships.

2. Empower Others by Sharing Ownership

One of the most powerful ways to foster collaboration and goodwill is to allow others to take ownership of ideas. When you let someone else feel that a concept or plan is partly their own, they become more invested and committed to its success. This approach not only encourages teamwork but also boosts the confidence and creativity of those around you. Instead of insisting on your ideas, create an environment where ideas can be shared and developed collectively. This not only leads to better outcomes but also strengthens your connections with others.

3. Acknowledge Your Mistakes Gracefully

Everyone makes mistakes, as imperfection is a natural aspect of life. What sets successful people apart is their ability to acknowledge their errors openly and sincerely. Admitting when you are wrong demonstrates humility and integrity, qualities that earn respect and trust from others. It also opens the door to learning and growth, allowing you to correct your course and improve in the future. By owning up to your mistakes, you not only resolve issues more effectively but also set a positive example for those around you.

4. Start Every Interaction with Kindness

First impressions are powerful, and the tone you set at the beginning of any interaction can significantly influence its outcome. Approaching others with warmth and friendliness creates a positive atmosphere that encourages open communication and mutual respect. Whether you're meeting someone for the first time or addressing a long-standing issue, beginning the conversation on a friendly note helps to disarm tension and build rapport. This approach not only makes others more receptive to your ideas but also fosters a more harmonious and supportive environment.

5. Listen More, Speak Less

In conversations, we naturally want to share our thoughts and opinions. However, true communication is about more than just talking—it's about listening. When you allow the other person to do most of the talking, you gain valuable insights into their thoughts, feelings, and motivations. This approach not only deepens your understanding of them but also ensures they feel appreciated and acknowledged. By engaging in active listening, you foster relationships that are rooted in trust and respect. Moreover, by speaking less, you can choose your words more carefully, making your contributions to the conversation more impactful.

The Psychology Behind Avoiding Arguments

At the heart of many arguments is the desire to be right and to assert one's dominance in a conversation. However, when emotions run high, rational thinking often takes a backseat, leading to escalation rather than resolution. Avoiding arguments doesn't mean shying away from important discussions; rather, it's about approaching disagreements with the goal of mutual understanding rather than victory. By doing so, you de-escalate potential conflicts and create an environment where productive dialogue can thrive.

Words of Wisdom: The safest way to get what you want is to deserve what you want.

– Wayne Dyer

Chapter 3

7 Major Time Wasters and How to Overcome Them

In the rapid pace of modern life, time is an immensely valuable asset. However, many of us find ourselves wasting it on activities that contribute little to our overall productivity. Identifying and addressing these time wasters can significantly enhance your effectiveness and satisfaction in life. Here's a look at seven common time wasters and strategies to overcome them.

1. Waiting for Inspiration

A prevalent habit is waiting for inspiration before taking action. Many people think that creativity and productivity depend on sudden flashes of inspiration, but this is rarely the case. This attitude can result in procrastination and missed chances.

Solution: Develop a routine that nurtures creativity and productivity. Establish a consistent schedule and set small, manageable goals to foster an environment conducive to inspiration. By consistently working on tasks, even without immediate inspiration, you build momentum that often leads to unexpected creative breakthroughs.

2. Repeating the Same Mistakes

Failing to learn from mistakes is a significant drain on both time and resources. When we do not address and learn from our errors, we remain stuck in a cycle of frustration and inefficiency, whether in personal projects, professional tasks, or relationships.

Solution: After making a mistake, analyze what went wrong and why. Create strategies to avoid recurring issues and foster a mindset of ongoing improvement. Actively seek out feedback to help refine and enhance your approach. This reflective approach helps transform mistakes into valuable learning experiences rather than recurring problems.

3. Always Complaining

Constant complaining can drain both time and energy, creating a negative atmosphere that affects personal well-being and team dynamics. Complaints often fail to address underlying issues and focus on the negatives.

Solution: Shift from complaining to problem-solving. When faced with challenges, identify practical steps to resolve them. Foster a positive mindset by practicing gratitude and celebrating small wins. This perspective shift can lead to greater resilience and more constructive outcomes.

4. Trying to Please Everybody

The urge to please everyone is a major time waster that can result in burnout and dissatisfaction. Overcommitting to meet everyone's expectations often detracts from focusing on your own priorities and can lead to ongoing stress.

Solution: Set clear boundaries and prioritize your own needs and goals. Recognize that it's impossible to satisfy everyone and focus on staying true to your own values and objectives. Communicate your boundaries assertively and concentrate on relationships and tasks that align with your personal goals.

5. Comparing Yourself

In today's social media-driven world, it's common to find yourself comparing your life to that of others. Constantly measuring your progress against others can lead to feelings of inadequacy and distract you from your own goals. This comparison often obscures your unique path and accomplishments.

Solution: Focus on comparing your progress to your own past performance rather than others. Set personal goals and track your growth using your own success metrics. Celebrate your achievements and use them as motivation instead of letting comparisons with others impact your self-esteem.

6. The Fear of Failure

The fear of failure can be immobilizing, stopping you from taking essential risks and grasping opportunities. This fear often leads to procrastination, avoidance, and missed growth opportunities, becoming a significant barrier to both personal and professional achievements.

Solution: Reframe failure as a learning experience rather than a setback. Adopt a growth mindset that views challenges as opportunities to develop new skills and gain valuable insights. Set achievable goals, take incremental steps toward them, and see failures as part of your journey toward success. Surround yourself with supportive individuals who encourage risk-taking and learning.

7. Expecting Perfectionism

Striving for perfection can be a major time waster, leading to endless revisions and delays. The pursuit of flawless results often causes procrastination and a fear of completing tasks, hindering progress and efficiency.

Solution: Set realistic and attainable standards for your work, understanding that perfection is often an unrealistic goal. Focus on delivering high-quality results without getting bogged down by minor imperfections. Embrace progress over perfection and recognize that achieving high standards is often more effective than chasing unattainable perfection.

Words of Wisdom: Better the foot slip than the tongue.

– Benjamin Franklin

Chapter 4

Know This Between 20-55 Years of Age

Life between the ages of 20 and 55 is a crucial period filled with opportunities for growth, challenges to overcome, and wisdom to gain. This stage of life often determines your future and is a time when you can shape the life you want. Here's what you should keep in mind during these years:

1. Take Care of Your Body

Your body is your most valuable possession. Throughout these years, it is critical to focus on your health because it is the basis for everything else in life. Regular exercise, a well-balanced diet, and adequate sleep are not simply habits; they are investments in the future of yourself. Remember that good health is a form of riches. Without it, all else is secondary.

2. Normalize Walking Some Paths Alone

Goals are deeply personal. As you go through life, you'll realize that not everyone understands or supports your goals. This is quite normal. Learn to walk some routes alone, focusing on your vision without seeking external validation.

3. Do not waste your energy on fear

Fear is a powerful feeling that might prevent you from fulfilling your potential. Instead of wasting energy on fear, redirect it into self-belief, gaining new skills, creating chances, and personal development. Fear can immobilize or motivate you.

4. Maintain a zero-expectation attitude towards others

Our happiness often depends on our expectations. The higher our expectations of others, the more likely we are to be disappointed. If you want to be truly happy, practice having no expectations from people. This is not to say that you should not care about people; it just means that your happiness should not be determined by their actions or acceptance.

5. Focus on Changing Yourself, not Others

Trying to change people is a useless undertaking that frequently results in frustration. Instead, consider how you interact with people and situations. Change your approach and mindset to retain your peace of mind and handle relationships more efficiently. Remember that you cannot control others, but you can control how you react to them.

6. Enjoy in the present moment and do whatever makes you happy

You won't stay young forever. Every day presents a chance to do something that makes you happy and fulfilled. Whether it's exploring a hobby, interacting with loved ones, or simply enjoying some peace, make an effort to do what makes you happy.

7. Manage your emotions

Being emotionally mature is an important component of personal development. Learn to regulate your emotions and respond less impulsively. This does not imply suppressing your feelings, but rather recognizing and responding constructively. Mastering your emotions can result in better decisions and greater relationships.

8. Free yourself from the norms of society

Society frequently imposes expectations and instructions on how people should live their lives. However, many of these expectations are based on out-of-date or irrelevant standards. Free yourself from societal guidance, especially if it contradicts your principles or ambitions. Remember, most people are still figuring things out on their own.

9. Align Yourself with Supportive People

Your social circle has a big impact on your success and well-being. Make sure your circle includes people who are proud of your accomplishments rather than jealous of them. Surround yourself with individuals who inspire you, support your goals, and foster your growth. Being around a positive and encouraging group can propel you toward new achievements.

10. Cultivate self-discipline and consistency

Self-discipline and consistency are crucial for success. These qualities significantly influence your career, personal goals, and relationships. By developing self-discipline and maintaining consistency, you'll see tangible improvements in your life. Success often stems from small, daily actions rather than grand gestures.

> **Words of Wisdom: You are not the slave of your past; you can transform your life the moment you make a choice.**
>
> **– Maxime Lagace**

Chapter 5

Memento Mori: The Reminder We All Desperately Need

We frequently fall prey to the chase of achievement, material possessions, and never-ending diversions in our fast-paced life. We frequently overlook the impermanence of existence and our own mortality. Memento Mori, a Latin term that means "remember that you must die," acts as a potent reminder to live in the present, prioritize what is truly important, and cherish life. This chapter examines the idea of Memento Mori and how it has significantly affected our lives.

What is Memento Mori?

The Latin expression "memento mori" means "remember that you must die" or "remember that you will die" in English. It is a philosophical idea that has existed throughout history, especially in the ancient Roman era and the Middle Ages. Memento Mori's stoicism acts as a reminder of the impermanence of life and the certainty of death. It nudges people to think about their death, ponder the transitoriness of life, and weigh the importance of time and their priorities. The memento mori symbol is used to remind people to appreciate the present moment and make the most of their lives while they still have them by encouraging them to live with more awareness, gratitude, and purpose.

Impact of Memento Mori on Our Lives

1. Accepting Impermanence

Memento Mori exhorts us to accept the transitory nature of life. It serves as a reminder that we are all doomed to the same end regardless of our accomplishments, riches, or social standing. Accepting this truth gives us a fresh outlook and enables us to recognise how valuable each day is.

2. Concentrating on What Really Matters

Material things and flimsy interests lose their meaning in the face of human mortality. We are prompted to consider our values and priorities by Memento Mori. It exhorts us to put our attention on fostering connections, developing personally, and making a positive difference in the world. We can live more content and meaningfully by focusing on what matters.

3. Living in the Present

Memento Mori serves as a reminder to always be in the present. We frequently overlook the beauty of the now when we are preoccupied with regrets from the past or worries about the future. By accepting our mortality, we get more conscious of the passing of time and are motivated to enjoy every moment.

4. Inspiration for Meaningful Activity

Memento Mori is a strong source of inspiration for meaningful activity. It forces us to push over our fears, apprehension, and self-doubt. We are motivated to achieve our aspirations, make a difference, and leave a lasting legacy because we are aware of how short our time is. It instills a sense of urgency and strengthens our drive to lead fulfilling lives.

The Importance of Memento Mori

1. Perspective

It's simple to lose sight of the wider picture when faced with our daily concerns and routines. Memento Mori shifts our perspective by serving as a poignant reminder of our mortality. It enables us to set priorities for what is important and let go of unimportant worries.

2. Gratitude

Memento Mori helps us develop a spirit of thanksgiving for the here and now and the people and things in our lives. We become more aware of the chances we have and the beauty around us when we recognise our limited time.

3. Reason

Pondering our mortality compels us to consider the significance and purpose of our life. It motivates us to live intentionally, maximize our time, and engage in pursuits that are consistent with our values and passions. Memento Mori is significant because it forces us to face our mortality, live in the present, and be mindful, grateful, and purposeful. It acts as a potent reminder to maximize our life and give priority to what is actually important.

Words of Wisdom: The problem is, you think you have time. On average, we get 80 summers... if we're lucky.

– Jack Kornfield

Chapter 6

7 Tough Truths You Must Embrace to Simplify Your Life

In our quest for a more fulfilling and less stressful life, we often overlook the hard truths that could lead us to profound change. Embracing these truths can help simplify your life and pave the way for genuine happiness and peace. Here are seven tough truths you need to confront to create a more straightforward and satisfying existence.

1. Others May Be Living Your Dream Life Because They Took Action

It's easy to feel envious of others who seem to have the life you desire, but the reality is that many of them got there simply because they took action. They might not be more talented or deserving; they just decided to pursue their goals. Understand that your aspirations are attainable if you venture beyond your comfort zone and take bold steps. Achieving your ideal life begins with taking one courageous step forward.

2. Forgiving Your Past Self Is Essential for Lasting Change

The weight of past mistakes and regrets can be a heavy burden that impedes your growth. To make meaningful and lasting changes, you must first forgive your past self. Holding onto guilt or self-blame keeps you anchored to old patterns and prevents you from moving forward. Embrace the fact that you're human and deserving of forgiveness, allowing yourself to release the past and focus on building a better future.

3. Shifting Your Perspective Can Change Your Life

You don't have to completely change your surroundings to discover happiness. Instead, focus on changing how you perceive your world. Your mindset has the power to influence how you experience life's challenges and joys. By shifting your perspective, you can find beauty and purpose in situations you once found frustrating or unfulfilling. Embrace this internal change to simplify your life and enhance your overall satisfaction.

4. Social media Can Divert Your Attention from an Unfulfilling Life

Social media can easily become a tool for escaping from an unsatisfying reality. It's often used to distract ourselves from our problems or dissatisfaction with life. By recognizing this pattern, you can take control of your social media usage and redirect your focus toward activities that genuinely enrich your life. Spend less time scrolling and more time engaging in meaningful activities that align with your values and goals.

5. Prioritizing What Matters Means Making Time for It

When something is truly important to you, you'll make it a priority and ensure you allocate time for it. Time management is less about finding time and more about prioritizing what you value most. Evaluate your schedule and identify what truly matters. If you're not dedicating time to your passions, relationships, or personal growth, it's time to reassess your priorities and make adjustments that reflect your genuine interests and goals.

6. Being Selfish Is Necessary for Self-Care

Self-care isn't a form of selfishness; it's an essential aspect of maintaining well-being. To be able to support and care for others effectively, you first need to address your own needs. Prioritizing self-care is essential for sustaining your well-being and maintaining your energy levels. By filling your own cup, you position yourself to offer more to those around you, creating a healthier and more balanced life. Embrace the concept of being selfish when it comes to self-care and personal growth.

7. The Step That Will Transform Your Life

The step you are most afraid of is often the one that holds the greatest potential for change. Fear typically arises when we're on the brink of stepping out of our comfort zones, and this fear can be a powerful indicator that a significant transformation is about to occur. Whether it's pursuing a new career, starting a challenging project, or making a major life decision, embracing that fear and taking the plunge can lead to profound personal and professional growth. By confronting and overcoming this fear, you unlock opportunities that might otherwise remain hidden, paving the way for a more fulfilling and enriched life.

Words of Wisdom: Don't just steal the style, steal the thinking behind the style.

– Hedy Lamarr

Chapter 7

7 Things Mentally Strong People Refuse to Do

Mental strength is not just about handling life's challenges but also about knowing what habits to avoid. People with mental resilience develop healthy thought patterns and behaviors that allow them to navigate difficult situations gracefully and effectively. What truly sets them apart are the things they consciously choose not to do. Below are seven behaviors that mentally strong people refuse to engage in, helping them maintain emotional balance and live fulfilling lives.

1. They Don't Give Away Their Power

Mentally strong individuals understand that no one can control their emotions, actions, or reactions unless they allow it. By refusing to give away their power, they maintain control over their lives. Whether it's dealing with criticism, unfair treatment, or hurtful words, mentally strong people choose how they respond. They avoid falling into the trap of blaming others for how they feel. By setting boundaries and maintaining self-control, they preserve their inner peace.

2. They Don't Shy Away from Change

Change is inevitable, but mentally strong people embrace it rather than resist it. They understand that personal growth often comes from adapting to new circumstances. Whether it's a career shift, moving to a new city, or navigating a challenging personal situation, mentally strong individuals view change as an opportunity rather than a threat. Their willingness to step out of their comfort zone allows them to evolve and improve continuously.

3. They Don't Fixate on What They Can't Change

Mentally strong people know the importance of focusing their energy on what they can control. They accept that certain situations are beyond their influence, such as other people's actions, unforeseen events, or past mistakes. Rather than wasting energy on trying to change what is out of their hands, they focus on their responses, actions, and decisions. This mindset prevents them from feeling overwhelmed by circumstances beyond their control and helps them channel their efforts into productive areas, leading to more positive outcomes.

4. They Don't Worry About Pleasing Everyone

Trying to please everyone is a futile effort that leads to stress, frustration, and a diluted sense of self. Mentally strong people recognize that it's impossible to meet everyone's expectations. Instead, they value authenticity and integrity more than seeking others' approval. They recognize that it's essential to say "no" to protect their mental and emotional health. By staying true to their values and focusing on what truly matters to them, they maintain healthier relationships and avoid the pitfalls of people-pleasing. In essence, they value quality over quantity when it comes to approval and connections.

5. They Don't Fear Taking Calculated Risks

Risk-taking is often associated with fear, but mentally strong people distinguish between reckless risks and calculated ones. They don't shy away from taking action because of fear. By trusting their judgment and doing thorough research, they build confidence in their ability to handle the outcomes—whether they succeed or fail. This willingness to embrace uncertainty helps them grow and achieve their goals without being held back by fear or doubt. Their calculated approach minimizes regret and opens doors to new opportunities.

6. They Don't Dwell on the Past

Everyone has experienced disappointments and failures in life, but mentally strong people refuse to let these define their future. They understand the value of learning from past mistakes, but they don't waste time ruminating over things they cannot change. Instead of fixating on past regrets or missed opportunities, they focus on what they can do better moving forward. By practicing forgiveness—both for themselves and others—they free up mental and emotional energy for growth. This proactive approach allows them to create new possibilities rather than remaining stuck in a cycle of guilt or blame.

7. They Avoid Repeating the Same Mistakes

Mentally strong people understand that mistakes are valuable learning tools, but only if lessons are learned and applied. They don't repeat the same errors because they make a conscious effort to reflect on their experiences and adjust their strategies. Whether it's in relationships, career decisions, or personal habits, they actively seek ways to improve and avoid falling into the same traps. They take responsibility for their actions and commit to self-growth by analyzing what went wrong and how they can do better in the future. This constant cycle of learning and improvement is a key factor in their resilience.

Words of Wisdom: Strength does not come from what you can do. It comes from overcoming the things you once thought you couldn't.

– Rikki Rogers

Section 2

Mastering Productivity and Personal Growth

During my college years, life seemed to move in slow, deliberate strides. My family didn't have much, and I had learned early on to make do with what was available. The most valuable possession I owned at the time was a single, worn-out pair of shoes. They were old, patched up from repeated use, and barely holding together. Yet, they were my only companions on long walks to the library, the endless hours spent poring over textbooks, and the even longer journeys to part-time jobs where I earned just enough to make ends meet.

One day, I found myself walking through campus, my shoes scuffing the pavement, when I overheard a group of students laughing at my shoes. Their mockery stung, but it wasn't the kind of sting that lingers in bitterness. Instead, it ignited something inside of me, a burning promise I made to myself. I silently told myself that this pair of shoes, this circumstance, would not define who I was or who I would become. I was determined not to let my current reality dictate my potential.

That was the moment that I began my journey toward self-improvement. I realized that success wasn't about the material wealth or the things I lacked—it was about how I chose to navigate life, especially in the face of adversity. I had no more excuses. I couldn't afford to wait for the perfect circumstances or the ideal situation. I needed to take control over what I could control: my mindset, my productivity, and my time. I began to read obsessively, learning everything I could about overcoming procrastination, maximizing my focus, and transforming my habits.

I also became a firm believer in the power of morning rituals. I had never thought of mornings as a sacred time until I stumbled upon a set of habits that transformed my day from the moment I opened my eyes. I started waking up before 7 AM, when the world around me was still quiet. I used that time to center myself. I exercised, meditated, and read, grounding myself for the challenges ahead. These rituals weren't just about productivity—they were about creating a mindset that set me up for success. They helped me build momentum each day, ensuring that my energy and focus were aligned with my goals.

With time, I began to see noticeable improvements in my life. I wasn't just getting by anymore—I was thriving. The morning rituals gave me the clarity and energy I needed to tackle my to-do list with fervor. But I needed more than just productivity tools. I needed strategies that would accelerate my personal growth, that would help me achieve ten times more than what I had been doing. That's when I found the concept of *10x improvement*. The idea is simple but profound: focus on doing things in a way that multiplies your efforts. Instead of working harder, I started to work smarter. I identified the activities that had the greatest impact on my life and focused most of my energy on those. By dedicating myself to continual improvement, I could achieve more in less time.

But in the pursuit of success, I also came to realize that not everything needed my attention. One of the hardest lessons I had to learn was how to overcome the toxic ego that can sabotage personal growth. My ego would often tell me I could do everything on my own or that I had to prove myself to everyone around me. But by learning to recognize and quiet that voice, I could focus on what truly mattered: my growth, my journey, and the impact I could make. Overcoming this ego was not just about letting go of pride; it was about embracing humility, being open to learning, and realizing that true success comes from a willingness to grow from every experience.

The journey was not without its challenges, but the lessons I learned were invaluable. The pair of shoes, though worn out, were my constant reminder that circumstances should never define us. They taught me the importance of overcoming procrastination, battling overthinking, and developing strategies that set me up for success. Today, I look back on that time with gratitude, knowing that every challenge was a stepping stone that led me to where I am now.

Chapter 8

My 7 Rules for Overcoming Procrastination

Procrastination is a common issue, but it mustn't be a major hurdle. By implementing these seven strategies, you can successfully tackle procrastination and boost your productivity.

1. Limit Learning Time

While continuous learning is crucial for growth, excessive learning without application can lead to procrastination. The key is to balance learning with application:

- **Learn and Apply:** For every hour you spend learning, dedicate an hour to applying what you've learned.

- **Avoid Overlearning:** Resist the urge to keep learning without putting your knowledge into practice. This approach ensures that you are not using learning as an excuse to procrastinate.

2. Adopt the 5-Minute Rule

This is often, the hardest part of any act is simply getting started. The 5-Minute Rule provides a simple but powerful method for addressing this challenge:

- **Set a 5-Minute Timer:** Perform a task you've been putting off and dedicate just five minutes to it.

- **Initiate the Task:** As soon as the timer starts, begin working on the task.

- **Decide After 5 Minutes:** You can stop or continue working once the five minutes are up. Most of the time, the momentum gained during these initial minutes will propel you to keep going, making it easier to complete the task.

3. Implement the 2-Minute Rule

The 2-Minute Rule is a quick way to deal with minor tasks that can otherwise become nagging distractions:

- **Handle Small Tasks Immediately:** If a task takes less than two minutes to complete, do it right away.

- **Clear Mental Clutter:** This approach prevents small tasks from accumulating and weighing on your mind.

4. Eat the Frog

The concept of "eating the frog" means tackling your most daunting task first:

- **Prioritize the Toughest Task:** Identify the most challenging task of your day and address it first.

- **Experience Relief:** Completing this task early frees you from the stress of having it loom over you.

- **Enjoy a Productive Day:** The rest of your day will feel more manageable in comparison.

5. Action Breeds Motivation

Many people believe that motivation precedes action. However, the opposite is often true:

- **Start with Small Actions:** Taking even the smallest step can create a sense of accomplishment.

- **Build Momentum:** This initial action can generate the motivation needed to tackle more significant tasks.

- **Keep the Momentum:** Taking small steps generates motivation, which then inspires further actions, creating a beneficial cycle.

6. Declutter Your Physical Space

A tidy environment contributes to a clear mind, making it easier to focus on your tasks:

Organize Your Workspace: Before starting work, ensure your surroundings are clean and organized.

Minimize Distractions: A clutter-free space helps you maintain concentration and improves overall productivity.

7. Eliminate Digital Clutter

Digital distractions are a significant source of procrastination. To stay focused, effectively manage your digital environment:

- **Airplane Mode:** Switch your phone to airplane mode to minimize interruptions.

- **Web Blockers:** Use tools like Cold Turkey to block distracting websites.

- **Relevant Tabs Only:** Keep only the tabs that are necessary for your current task open.

Integrating these seven strategies into your daily routine can greatly diminish procrastination and boost your productivity. Each technique targets a particular facet of procrastination, offering a well-rounded method for overcoming it. Begin with small steps, stay consistent, and observe how your focus and task-completion skills improve over time.

Words of Wisdom: Discipline is the bridge between goals and accomplishment.

– Jim Rohn

Chapter 9

Powerful Strategies to Conquer Overthinking

Overthinking can be a silent yet debilitating struggle, often leading to anxiety, stress, and missed opportunities. By adopting a few key strategies, you can regain control over your thoughts and foster a more positive mindset. Here are five effective techniques to assist you in overcoming, overthinking and achieving a more harmonious life.

1. Recognize That the Real Problem Is Often in Your Mind

Many times, we create problems in our minds that don't truly exist. In fact, about 99% of the distress we experience is self-inflicted, stemming from our own thoughts and perceptions. Only a small fraction, approximately 1%, comes from the actual situation or outcome. This means that the way we interpret challenges often causes more harm than the challenges themselves. Instead of fixating on what might go wrong, try to identify the narrative you've built around the problem. By shifting your focus from the issue itself to your perception of it, you can begin to dismantle the mental barriers that hold you back.

2. Stop Sabotaging Yourself with Self-Rejection

When opportunities arise, many people hesitate, thinking they aren't worthy or capable. For instance, if you're uncertain about your qualifications for a job, apply anyway. And if you think there's little chance of receiving a response to your email, send it without hesitation. Avoid allowing overthinking to morph into self-rejection. Embrace the possibility of success by taking action, even when doubt creeps in.

3. Verify Your Thoughts with Reality

Our minds often conjure up scenarios influenced by our insecurities and fears, leading us to believe in narratives that may not be true. This is particularly prevalent in emotionally charged situations. To combat this tendency, it's crucial to fact-check your thoughts. Before accepting any negative belief, ask yourself whether it's based on evidence or merely a reflection of your worries. Engaging in this critical examination can help you gain clarity and allow you to separate fact from fiction.

4. Find Peace Through Acceptance

Many of us struggle with anxiety about the future and regret about the past, believing that these feelings will somehow change our circumstances. However, peace is often found in acceptance. Understand that no amount of worry will alter what's to come, nor will dwelling on past mistakes change what has already occurred. Embrace the idea that imperfection is part of life, that uncertainty is inevitable, and that some things are beyond your control. By accepting these realities, you can release the burden of overthinking and find a more tranquil state of mind.

5. Prioritize Mental Health for Overall Well-Being

Physical health is vital, but it's equally important to address the mental aspect. You might engage in exercise, eat healthily, practice yoga, stay hydrated, and take supplements, but without confronting the negativity in your thoughts, achieving true health will remain elusive. Mental well-being plays a crucial role in your overall health, so make it a priority to address negative thinking patterns. Incorporate practices such as mindfulness, meditation, or cognitive behavioral strategies to cultivate a healthier mindset. By nurturing your mental health, you can create a solid foundation for physical wellness.

Words of Wisdom: Clarity isn't about knowing what you want to do with your life, it's about knowing what you want to do this week. You don't need to have it all figured out. You just need to know your next step.

– Mel Robbins

Chapter 10

How to Become a Productivity Master: The 60/10 Method

The ability to maximize productivity is crucial for success in today's fast-paced world. With so many responsibilities and distractions, finding a productive way to increase your output becomes essential. The 60/10 strategy is one such approach that is gaining acceptance.

The 60/10 method is a time-management strategy that emphasizes switching between periods of focused work and quick breaks. It entails committing 60 minutes of concentrated work to a particular task, followed by a 10-minute rest period. This strategy's main goal is to utilize the power of intense concentration during work sprints while providing for appropriate breaks to avoid burnout.

How to Apply the 60/10 Method

1. Establish Specific Objectives:

Begin by outlining specific goals for each work session. You'll be more motivated and able to maintain your focus for the entire 60 minutes if you have a clear goal in mind.

2. Eliminate Distractions:

Reduce distractions by turning off notifications, removing useless tabs, and establishing a productive workspace. Getting rid of distractions will improve your capacity to focus on the current activity.

3. Deep Work Mode:

As soon as the 60-minute work sprint starts, go into deep work mode. This entails focusing all your attention and effort on the subject without multitasking or flitting between various tasks. Put quality before quantity.

4. Take Consistent Breaks:

After the 60-minute work session, give yourself a 10-minute break to relax and recover. Make use of this opportunity to stretch, drink some water, or perform a small activity that relaxes and renews your mind.

5. Rinse and Repeat:

Repeat the cycle of 60 minutes of concentrated work and 10 minutes of breaks throughout your workday. Change the intervals depending on your tastes and energy levels, but keep consistency in following the routine.

The Advantages of the 60/10 Method

Increased Foc54r3es2wqaus:

You may dive deeply into activities and keep a high focus by setting aside uninterrupted blocks of time to work, boosting productivity and efficiency.

Improved Energy Management:

Regular breaks throughout the day keep energy levels up and help prevent burnout. Your brain can recover and avoid mental tiredness with brief rest times.

Time management:

Time management is improved since you can better understand how long tasks take to complete and can schedule your day accordingly. This approach promotes prioritization and efficient time management.

Enhanced Productivity:

You can establish a rhythm that increases productivity system by planning your work intervals and including brief breaks. The methodical technique enables you to maximize your productivity.

Words of Wisdom: You practice and you get better. It's very simple.

– Gail Devers

Chapter 11

5 Powerful Morning Rituals to Start Before 7 AM

If you're looking to boost productivity, energy levels, and overall well-being, establishing a solid morning routine is essential. By adopting healthy habits before the clock hits 7 AM, you can create a foundation for success. Let's explore five powerful rituals you can incorporate into your early mornings to enhance focus and set a positive tone for the rest of your day.

1. Hydrate First Thing and Refresh Your Mind

One of the simplest yet most effective morning rituals is to drink water right after waking up. After several hours of sleep, your body becomes dehydrated, and replenishing it with water is crucial. Drinking water in the morning not only helps kickstart your metabolism but also aids in flushing out toxins, giving you a refreshing boost of energy.

This small step can make a huge difference in how you feel throughout the day. You'll be more alert, more focused, and better prepared to tackle the tasks ahead. Pair this ritual with a few moments to freshen up by washing your face or brushing your teeth, and you'll instantly feel revitalized and ready to take on the morning.

2. Keep Your Smartphone at Bay

In a world where technology plays such a prominent role, it can be tempting to check your smartphone immediately upon waking. However, this habit can lead to stress and distraction before your day even begins. Checking emails, social media, or news headlines right away can overwhelm your mind and steer your focus in the wrong direction.

Instead, make an effort to stay away from your phone for at least the first hour after waking up. Allow yourself the mental space to ease into the day without external influences. You'll find that your mood is more balanced, and you have a clearer mind to focus on what truly matters—your goals and priorities. Reserve screen time for after you've completed your morning rituals to preserve your focus.

3. Get Moving with a 30-Minute Workout

Exercise is an excellent way to boost both physical and mental energy, and it doesn't have to be long or complicated. A 30-minute workout in the morning can significantly improve your mood, increase your productivity, and sharpen your mental clarity. Whether it's a run, yoga session, or home workout, physical activity releases endorphins that enhance your sense of well-being.

Exercise in the morning also sets the tone for healthy decisions throughout the day. It reminds you to fuel your body properly and motivates you to remain active. Even if it's a brisk walk or light stretching, getting your body moving before 7 AM can lead to long-term benefits for both your mind and body.

4. Practice 10 Minutes of Meditation and Take a Refreshing Shower

Once you've got your body moving, it's time to focus on your mental well-being. Carving out 10 minutes to meditate can help you clear your mind, reduce stress, and set a positive intention for the day. Meditation promotes mindfulness and helps you stay present, making it easier to handle challenges and distractions throughout the day.

After meditating, take a refreshing shower to complete the ritual. Showers not only cleanse the body but can also provide mental clarity. A cold or lukewarm shower can stimulate blood flow and further boost your energy levels, leaving you feeling invigorated and ready to face whatever comes your way.

5. Review Your Daily Goals and Plan Your Day

The final ritual before officially starting your day should be reviewing your goals and planning your schedule. Taking a few minutes to outline your priorities ensures that you stay focused and organized. Whether you use a planner, journal, or digital tool, jotting down your top tasks for the day gives you a clear direction.

Reflect on both your short-term and long-term goals. Having this sense of purpose will help you approach your day with confidence and motivation. By clarifying your intentions in the morning, you'll feel more in control and better equipped to manage your time effectively.

Words of Wisdom: Keep going, because the best is yet to come. Keep going, because you're stronger than you think you are.

— **Brian Tracy**

Chapter 12

5 Powerful Strategies to Achieve 10x Improvement Every Day

We all aspire to be better versions of ourselves, but transforming into someone who is consistently ten times better each day requires a proactive approach. By incorporating a few powerful habits into your daily routine, you can significantly enhance your productivity, mindset, and overall well-being. Here are five transformative strategies to help you achieve exponential growth every day.

1. Embrace Daily Self-Reflection

Self-reflection is more than just a moment of introspection; it's a crucial practice for understanding your daily progress and areas for improvement. Reflect on your actions, decisions, and interactions, identifying patterns that contribute to your success or setbacks. This practice allows you to learn from your experiences, make necessary adjustments, and continuously evolve.

To make self-reflection effective, consider keeping a journal where you can jot down your thoughts and insights. By regularly reviewing these entries, you can track your growth, celebrate your achievements, and address any recurring challenges. This habit not only helps you become more self-aware but also empowers you to take actionable steps towards becoming 10x better each day.

2. Commit to Reading a Chapter Daily

Committing to reading a chapter from a book every day fosters a routine of gaining new insights and expanding your knowledge. Select books that resonate with your interests, objectives, or areas where you aim to improve.

Whether it's a business book, a self-help guide, or a novel, reading stimulates your mind, broadens your understanding, and enhances your creativity. It also serves as a productive escape from daily stresses, providing you with fresh insights and ideas. Over time, this daily reading habit will contribute significantly to your intellectual growth and overall development.

3. Dedicate Time for Solitude

In our fast-paced world, finding time for solitude can be incredibly rejuvenating. Allocate at least thirty minutes each day for quiet reflection, meditation, or simply being alone with your thoughts. This period gives you the opportunity to clear your thoughts, alleviate stress, and gain insight into your priorities and objectives.

Solitude is not about isolation but about creating space for self-care and mental rejuvenation. During this period, you can participate in activities that promote relaxation and rejuvenation, such as practicing deep breathing, writing in a journal, or simply enjoying a quiet moment. By making solitude a part of your daily routine, you'll enhance your focus, decision-making abilities, and overall emotional well-being.

4. Set and Achieve Small Daily Goals

Goal-setting is a powerful motivator, and breaking down your larger objectives into smaller, manageable tasks can drive daily progress. Each day, set a specific, achievable goal for yourself and work towards accomplishing it. These goals could range from completing a work task, learning a new skill, or engaging in a healthy habit.

The secret to achieving success with this approach is to make sure your daily objectives are both attainable and quantifiable. By accomplishing these small goals, you build momentum and confidence, which contributes to your overall growth and development. Celebrate your daily achievements, no matter how small, as they contribute to your journey of becoming 10x better every day.

5. Challenge Yourself to Learn Something New

Make it a daily challenge to acquire new knowledge or skills, whether it's through online courses, tutorials, or practical experiences. This habit keeps your mind sharp and opens up new development opportunities.

Learning something new each day doesn't have to be a major undertaking; it could be as simple as exploring a new topic of interest, practicing a new skill, or staying updated with industry trends. Embrace curiosity and approach each day with a willingness to expand your horizons. Over time, this commitment to learning will enhance your capabilities, boost your confidence, and contribute to your overall improvement.

Words of Wisdom: If you want to poison a village, poison their well. But if you want to poison people, poison their stories. Because stories sway people.

– Diana Wynne Jones

Chapter 13

How to Get Your Life Back on Track

Life can often feel overwhelming, leaving us feeling stuck and unable to move forward. Whether you're grappling with personal challenges, career setbacks, or simply feeling lost, there are steps you can take to regain control and get your life back on track.

1. Take Charge of Your Life

The first step toward regaining control is to stop adopting a victim mentality. Life is filled with challenges, and it's easy to feel like circumstances are working against you. While it's true that not everything that happens is within our control, how we respond to adversity is entirely our choice. Rather than fighting against the realities of life, accept and welcome them. Acknowledge disappointments, learn from your experiences, and focus on how you can shape a brighter future. Taking responsibility for your life empowers you to navigate challenges with resilience.

2. Reframe Your Perspective on Circumstances

Next, it's essential to shift your mindset regarding your circumstances. Imagine success measured by financial stability. Some individuals start their journey with ample resources, while others have to build from scratch. What truly matters is how we respond to our situations. While we may not be able to control the challenges that come our way, we do have the power to shape our responses and our resolve to tackle them. Understand that success often favors those who concentrate on what they can influence rather than those who dwell on the uncontrollable aspects of life. Focus on proactive solutions rather than external factors that may hinder your progress.

3. Recognize Hard Work Over Luck

It's common to label successful individuals as "lucky," but this mindset can be detrimental. Research shows that a significant percentage of wealthy individuals come from middle-income backgrounds rather than privileged ones. A mere 2% of millionaires are born into wealth. When we attribute success to luck, we undermine the hard work, learning, and perseverance that these individuals have invested in their journeys. Instead of envying others' achievements, shift your focus to what you can learn from their stories. Acknowledge that success is often the result of dedication, resilience, and an unwavering commitment to one's goals.

4. Cultivate Self-Compassion

It's vital to avoid falling into the trap of self-pity. Take a moment to examine your surroundings and the roles of the various elements in your life. Every person, situation, and challenge has a purpose in your personal narrative. Your journey is shaped by the ability to keep moving forward, regardless of setbacks. Embrace the idea that life is a series of ups and downs, and the key to success lies in your ability to persist. The moment you decide to stop trying is when you truly fail. So, remind yourself to keep pushing forward and to maintain a positive attitude toward your journey.

5. Get Back Up After Setbacks

Life is filled with obstacles, but these challenges should be viewed as opportunities for growth rather than as punishments. Embrace the discomfort that comes with facing difficulties; they can serve as powerful catalysts for personal development. Much like the process of strength training, which involves breaking down and rebuilding muscles, confronting challenges is essential for success. If you allow yourself to remain down after a setback, you risk letting fear of failure triumph over your desire for success. Remember, the most significant victories often come from rising after a fall and learning from the experience.

Words of Wisdom: Maybe the journey isn't about becoming anything. Maybe it's about unbecoming everything that isn't really you, so that you can be who you were meant to be in the first place.

– Paulo Coelho

Chapter 14

How to Find Your Circle of Genius

We all have unique talents and qualities that distinguish us. Recognizing and fostering these innate gifts is the first step on our path to personal fulfillment and success. Finding your zone of genius becomes critical in the pursuit of your dreams. It is the place where our interests meet our skills, allowing us to soar to new heights and make a significant difference in our lives and the world around us.

Understanding the Circle of Genius

Your circle of genius depicts the meeting point of your interests, talents, and strengths. It is the state of being where you are passionately engaged, energized, and easily capable. When you operate within your circle of genius, time seems to fly by, and you enter a state of flow in which everything falls into place flawlessly.

Identifying Your Interests

Passions are the driving force that pulls us ahead. They are the activities, topics, or causes that pique our interest and make us feel alive. Spend some time thinking about what excites you. What hobbies do you enjoy that cause you to lose track of time? What themes do you naturally gravitate towards? Identifying your passions will provide you with a solid foundation for investigating your circle of brilliance.

Discovering Your Strengths and Talents

Your talents and strengths are your natural abilities. They are the things you succeed at easily or with little effort. Consider your previous accomplishments and feedback from others to find your talents and strengths. What abilities do people frequently congratulate you on? What chores do you find straightforward to complete? Investigating your talents and strengths will assist you in identifying areas where you have a natural advantage.

Finding Harmony

It's time to find congruence between your passions, abilities, and strengths now that you've identified them. Look for opportunities where your interests and skills connect. These are the areas where you can flourish by leveraging your unique abilities. Consider how you can use your talents and knowledge to make a difference in the areas that pique your interest. You can enter your circle of genius by aligning your passions and talents.

Accepting Change and Continuous Learning

Finding your circle of genius is a journey that necessitates ongoing development and learning. Be open to new experiences and opportunities to increase your knowledge and skills as you explore your areas of alignment. Accept challenges and see them as opportunities to progress. Seek feedback and guidance to help you improve your skills. You will continue evolving within your genius circle by adopting a growth mindset and constantly honing your talents.

Overcoming Obstacles and Fears

You may face hurdles and worries as you seek to explore your circle of genius. Doubt, fear of failure, and societal expectations can all hinder our growth. It is critical to understand that failures and challenges are a normal part of the trip and should not discourage you.

Accept resilience and tenacity, and see obstacles as chances for growth. Surround yourself with a supportive network of people who believe in your abilities and can offer advice and encouragement.

Making a Difference

When you work within your circle of genius, you feel personal fulfillment and have the chance to impact the world around you positively. You can contribute to causes aligning with your values and effect significant change by harnessing your talents and passions. Your circle of genius allows you to create a lasting impact through your career, creative hobbies, or community activity.

Finding your circle of brilliance is a personal journey that contains the secret to realizing your most significant potential and living a meaningful life. It entails identifying your passions, abilities, and strengths and aligning them to allow you to perform at your best. You will feel a sense of fluidity, engagement, and the capacity to influence this environment greatly.

Words of Wisdom: Success is not the key to happiness. Happiness is the key to success. If you love what you are doing, you will be successful.

– Albert Schweitzer

Chapter 15

5 Ways to Overcome the Toxic Ego That Can Wreck Your Life

Ego can be a double-edged sword; while it can motivate us, it can also lead to destructive behaviors and harmful mindsets. A toxic ego can cloud judgment, create conflict, and sabotage our relationships. If you find that your ego is holding you back from living your best life, consider these five strategies to help you transcend it.

1. Embrace Action Over Talk

It's easy to get caught up in discussions, making grand plans or declarations about what you intend to do. However, this often leads to inaction and a false sense of accomplishment. Instead of merely talking about your ambitions, focus on tangible steps you can take. Action is what truly drives progress. When you shift your energy from talking to doing, you will start to see results and feel a sense of fulfillment that mere conversation cannot provide. Dive into your tasks, commit to your goals, and let your actions speak louder than words.

2. Release the Need for Validation

In a world driven by likes, shares, and accolades, it's tempting to seek validation through external recognition. However, chasing credit can feed your ego and distract you from what truly matters. Let go of the need for applause and appreciation. Instead, focus on the intrinsic rewards of your efforts. Evaluate your accomplishments based on personal growth and satisfaction rather than how others perceive them. By doing so, you'll cultivate a sense of self-worth that doesn't depend on external validation, fostering a healthier mindset.

3. Recognize When to Step Back

We've all experienced moments when things don't go as planned, leading us into a downward spiral. In these instances, it's essential to recognize when to pause and reassess. If you find yourself entrenched in a negative situation, resist the urge to dig deeper in hopes of finding a solution. Sometimes, it's more beneficial to change direction rather than persist in a losing battle. Allow yourself the space to breathe, reassess your options, and find a more constructive path forward.

4. Prioritize Love Over Fear

A toxic ego often stems from fear—fear of rejection, failure, or inadequacy. Opt to respond with compassion instead of defensiveness. When faced with challenges or conflicts, ask yourself what a loving response would look like. Prioritizing love allows you to foster positive connections, improve your emotional well-being, and dissolve the barriers that your ego has built. Love not only nurtures relationships but also cultivates resilience in the face of adversity.

5. Shift Your Focus from Image to Purpose

In our appearance-driven society, it's easy to get caught up in how we present ourselves to the world. This fixation on images can distract us from our true purpose and values. Instead of worrying about how others perceive you, redirect your energy toward a higher purpose. By focusing on significant contributions and ensuring your actions align with your true purpose, you can reduce the impact of your ego. This shift in perspective can lead to a more fulfilling life, where your self-worth is defined by your impact rather than your image.

Words of Wisdom: You've got to be a thermostat rather than a thermometer. A thermostat shapes the climate of opinion; a thermometer just reflects it.

– Jim Rohn

Chapter 16

The Locus Rule: How to Control Your Life

Life is an adventure full of options and decisions. External circumstances may appear to have a grasp on our lives at times, but each of us possesses the ability to determine our own destiny. Based on the internal locus of control concept, the Locus Rule empowers us to take charge of our lives, embrace personal responsibility, and make our aspirations a reality.

The Locus Rule Explained

The Locus Rule is based on the concept of the locus of control, which is the assumption that we can affect and control the results of our lives. Instead of blaming our success or failure on external forces, the Locus Rule encourages us to take responsibility for our actions, decisions, and mindset.

Accepting Personal Responsibility

Accepting personal responsibility for our lives is the first step towards living by the Locus Rule. It entails taking that, regardless of our circumstances, we have the ability to shape our own future. We reclaim control over our lives and become the builders of our own success by taking ownership of our thoughts, emotions, and behaviors.

The Transition from Victimhood to Empowerment

Adopting the Locus Rule necessitates a mental shift—from viewing ourselves as victims of circumstance to recognizing our inherent power and action. We must abandon the assumption that external forces control our lives and instead concentrate on what we can do to effect positive change. Recognizing that we maintain our responses and attitudes liberates us from victimhood and opens the path to empowerment.

Creating a Growth Mindset

A developmental mentality is required to follow the Locus Rule. The concept is that hard work, dedication, and a desire to learn can increase our abilities and intelligence. We see challenges as chances for progress and setbacks as stepping stones to success when we have a growth mindset.

We increase our potential and accelerate ourselves toward our goals by establishing a perspective focused on constant improvement.

Setting Meaningful Objectives

To effectively utilize the Locus Rule, we must first establish meaningful goals that are in line with our beliefs and aspirations. We give ourselves direction and purpose by identifying clear objectives. Create an action plan to reach your goals by breaking them down into minor, more doable ones. Remember that it is within your hands to work tirelessly towards your goals and to adapt as needed.

Resilience and Adaptability Development

Living by the Locus Rule necessitates adaptability and tenacity. Surprising twists and turns are common in life as a whole and failures are inevitable. However, by cultivating resilience, we are able to recover from challenges and setbacks, learning from them and using them as stepping stones towards growth. Adaptability permits us to modify our strategies and approach when confronted with a challenge.

Surrounding Yourself with Encouragement

When applying the Locus Rule, it is critical to have supportive relationships. Surround yourself with people who believe in your potential, push you to grow, and encourage you along the way. Seek out mentors, join communities, and participate in networking opportunities that are relevant to your goals. Collaborating with like-minded people improves your resolve and supports your trust in the Locus Rule's potency.

Words of Wisdom: Between stimulus and response, there is a space. In that space is our power to choose our response. In our response lies our growth and our freedom.

– Viktor E. Frankl

Chapter 17

6 Essential Boundaries Everyone Should Establish

Establishing healthy boundaries is essential for ensuring emotional wellness and nurturing positive relationships. Boundaries help you define what is acceptable for you and what is not, allowing you to protect your emotional, physical, and mental space.

1. Emotional Boundaries

Emotional boundaries involve understanding your limits regarding emotional involvement with others. It's vital to recognize when you can support someone without taking on their emotional burdens, especially when you're already at capacity. Learn to avoid discussions or topics that trigger negative feelings for you, and make a conscious effort to separate your emotions from those of others. By prioritizing your emotional health, you enable yourself to engage in supportive relationships without losing yourself in the process.

2. Relationship Boundaries

Relationship boundaries dictate how you expect to be treated by others and what behaviors are acceptable around you. This includes setting standards for how you want people to communicate with you and what you will tolerate in terms of respect and support. Clearly define your needs and expectations in your relationships, whether they are romantic, platonic, or professional. By doing so, you cultivate mutual respect and understanding, ensuring that your relationships remain healthy and fulfilling.

3. Physical Boundaries

Physical boundaries relate to your personal space and the right to control your physical autonomy. It's essential to determine who is allowed to enter your personal space, how close someone can get to you, and what type of physical contact you are comfortable with. Additionally, these boundaries extend to what you choose to put into your body, including food and drink. Establishing clear physical boundaries empowers you to protect your body and comfort, ensuring that interactions are consensual and respectful.

4. Communication Boundaries

Communication boundaries involve the rules you set regarding how you interact verbally with others and how they communicate with you. This includes acceptable language, tone, and topics of discussion. It's crucial to express what you find disrespectful or unacceptable in conversations. Additionally, practice speaking to yourself with kindness and respect, as your inner dialogue significantly impacts your self-esteem. Setting communication boundaries encourages more positive interactions, cultivates mutual respect, and facilitates open discussions.

5. Mental Boundaries

Mental boundaries involve giving yourself the freedom to hold your own thoughts, beliefs, and opinions, even if they differ from those of others. It's essential to feel comfortable expressing your views without fear of judgment or conflict. Recognize that it's okay for others to disagree with you; this acceptance can enhance your relationships and encourage healthy debates. By setting mental boundaries, you assert your right to think freely and shield your mind from unwarranted influence.

6. Time Boundaries

Time boundaries revolve around how you allocate your time and how others should respect your schedule. This includes setting limits on how much time you spend with others and communicating your availability for social engagements or work commitments. It's important to be clear about your boundaries concerning lateness, last-minute requests, and obligations that may infringe on your time. Focusing on your time management enables you to achieve a better balance between work and personal life, ensuring that your obligations are in harmony with your personal aspirations.

Words of Wisdom: When people talk, listen completely. Most people never listen.

– Ernest Hemingway

Section 3

Wisdom and Resilience in Adversity

Life is a relentless teacher, imparting wisdom through trials and tribulations. My journey is a testament to how resilience, sacrifice, and unyielding determination can illuminate the darkest paths. Here, I share moments etched in my memory—moments of profound adversity that shaped my character and instilled in me the strength to persevere.

In my 12th grade, the cost of education became a mountain we had to climb. My parents had exhausted all resources, and as a last resort, they sold the last piece of gold we owned to purchase my books. It wasn't enough. My mother and father, desperate to support my education, turned to our neighbor for help. She lent us ₹50,000 at a staggering interest rate of ₹750 per month. The weight of this decision was heavy—both financially and emotionally. For the next six and a half years, we lived under the shadow of debt, ultimately paying ₹58,500 in interest alone. Yet, this sacrifice was a profound lesson in prioritizing knowledge over material possessions.

The following year, when I was accepted into college, a new challenge emerged. The admission required ₹45,000—an impossible amount given our financial constraints. Having already borrowed from the neighboring aunty, we couldn't approach her again. My mother, a house help, shared our predicament with her employers. Their large-hearted family managed to pool together ₹20,000, but we were still short ₹25,000. My mother made an unthinkable decision—she sold her cherished mangalsutra, a symbol of her marriage, for ₹30,000. She replaced it with an artificial one worth ₹5,000, smiling through her pain and reassuring me that my future was worth every sacrifice.

Through persistence and effort, I had secured a commendable All India Rank in the engineering entrance exams. Yet, even with this achievement, the financial burden of higher education loomed large. Recognizing our circumstances, I sought a scholarship offered by University for students from weaker sections. The process was nerve-wracking. I vividly remember accompanying my father to Kashmere Gate, where we presented our case before the jury panel. Those moments of vulnerability were humbling, but I left with immense gratitude when the scholarship was approved. It wasn't just financial aid—it was a lifeline.

Growing up, even basic amenities were a luxury. Our home lacked a personal washroom, and each morning began with a long wait in line at the community washroom. It was an experience that tested patience and endurance. While many take such conveniences for granted, those queues taught me resilience, humility, and the value of small comforts.

Looking back on those early years of my educational journey, I recognize how easy it would have been to succumb to the ***Dunning-Kruger Effect***, believing that I was incapable of overcoming these monumental financial barriers. In my youth, I might have overestimated my own limitations, assuming that certain goals were too far out of reach. However, what I learned in those challenging years is that true capability is revealed when we push beyond our perceived boundaries. The process of constantly striving—no matter the odds—showed me that our real potential often becomes evident only when we persist in the face of overwhelming doubt. Each time we faced a new obstacle, I learned that true mastery comes from humility and the willingness to learn from our challenges.

The lessons of humility, gratitude, and perseverance have become my guiding principles. Adversity may challenge us, but it also strengthens us, revealing a reservoir of wisdom and resilience we never knew existed. Through every hardship, I learned that true wealth lies not in possessions but in the courage to dream and the determination to turn those dreams into reality.

Chapter 18

The Cockroach Theory for Self-Development

We frequently seek comfort and avoid situations that make us uncomfortable in our pursuit of personal growth and self-development. True change, on the other hand, comes from embracing discomfort and confronting our fears head-on. The Cockroach Theory, based on a simple comparison, teaches us important lessons about tenacity, adaptability, and the value of stepping outside of our comfort zones.

Understanding the Cockroach Theory

The Cockroach Theory is a metaphor that implies that troubles and unpleasant events are akin to cockroaches. It emphasizes how, like a concealed infestation, avoiding or ignoring these difficulties helps them to endure and grow. However, tackling these issues head-on reduces their power over us, and we can effectively handle and conquer them.

The Cockroach Theory, at its foundation, advocates embracing discomfort as a motivator for human growth. It inspires people to move beyond their comfort zones and face difficult situations with courage and resilience. This allows one to learn new talents, gain experience, and broaden their personal capabilities.

Benefits of Cockroach Theory for Self-Development

1. Embracing Discomfort:

When confronted with challenges or uncomfortable situations, our impulse may be to flee or avoid them. The Cockroach Theory, on the other hand, teaches us the value of embracing discomfort. We can develop resilience and overcome impediments to our personal progress by admitting and confronting our anxieties. Pain allows us to learn, adapt, and become better versions of ourselves.

2. Taking a Risk:

Our comfort zones are secure and familiar but may also be restricting. The Cockroach Theory challenges us to leave our comfort zones and venture into unexplored territory. We expose ourselves to new experiences, ideas, and viewpoints in this way, which might lead to personal growth. We find our full potential and open up new possibilities when uncomfortable with the unknown.

3. Learning from failures:

Failure is unavoidable, and the Cockroach Theory reminds us that it is not something to dread or avoid. On the other hand, failure should be viewed as an excellent learning opportunity. When we face setbacks or make mistakes, we can view them as stepping stones towards growth. We can progress and reach our goals by analysing our failures, grasping the lessons they teach us, and making the required modifications.

4. Building Resilience:

The Cockroach Theory emphasises the necessity of resilience as a vital quality for personal development. Stability enables us to recover, adapt, and continue when confronted with difficulties, setbacks, or unpleasant conditions. We cultivate the ability to navigate life's ups and downs with grace and drive by cultivating resilience. Overcoming adversity allows us to develop character and emerge stronger than before.

5. Embracing Change:

Change is an unavoidable element of life, and the Cockroach Theory encourages us to accept change rather than reject it. We open ourselves to new opportunities and progress by taking and adapting to change. Change can be uncomfortable and disruptive, but it also provides opportunities to reinvent ourselves, develop new skills, and explore new avenues. Accepting change allows us to grow and broaden our horizons.

Words of Wisdom: Suffering only comes from not making decisions, not by making wrong decisions.

– Roberto Assagioli

Chapter 19

The Dunning-Kruger Effect: An Overestimation of Capability

In the realm of human cognition, our ability to assess our own competence is often biased and prone to misjudgment. The Dunning-Kruger Effect, a psychological phenomenon identified by social psychologists David Dunning and Justin Kruger in 1999, reveals how individuals with low ability in a particular domain tend to overestimate their competence, while those with high ability often underestimate theirs.

Understanding the Dunning-Kruger Effect

The Dunning-Kruger Effect stems from a cognitive bias that impairs our self-awareness and skews our self-assessment of competence. It manifests as a tendency for individuals of low ability to hold overly optimistic views of their own skills and knowledge in a given domain, leading them to believe they are more competent than they actually are. Conversely, individuals with high competence may underestimate their abilities, assuming that others possess a similar level of proficiency.

The phenomenon arises due to a two-fold cognitive distortion: lack of metacognitive skills and a limited understanding of the domain itself. Those with lower abilities may lack the knowledge and expertise necessary to recognize their own deficiencies, hindering their ability to accurately assess their performance. Additionally, their limited understanding of the domain prevents them from recognizing the complexities and nuances involved, leading to an inflated sense of competence.

Implications and Challenges

The Dunning-Kruger Effect has significant implications across various aspects of life:

1. **Decision-Making:** Individuals influenced by the Dunning-Kruger Effect may make poor decisions due to their unwarranted confidence. They may overlook critical information, dismiss expert advice, and underestimate the risks involved, leading to suboptimal outcomes.

2. **Skill Development:** The overestimation of competence can hinder personal growth and skill development. Those afflicted by the Dunning-Kruger Effect may perceive themselves as already highly skilled, reducing their motivation to improve or seek further knowledge and feedback.

3. **Interpersonal Relationships:** Misjudging one's competence can strain interpersonal relationships. Individuals with inflated self-perceptions may disregard the perspectives and expertise of others, leading to conflicts, poor teamwork, and an overall breakdown in collaboration.

Overcoming the Dunning-Kruger Effect

Awareness and self-reflection are crucial in mitigating the impact of the Dunning-Kruger Effect. Here are some strategies to help individuals overcome this cognitive bias:

1. **Seek Objective Feedback:** Actively solicit feedback from knowledgeable and unbiased sources to gain a realistic perspective

on your abilities. External evaluations can provide valuable insights and highlight areas for improvement.

2. **Cultivate Humility:** Recognize that expertise is a lifelong journey and embrace a mindset of continuous learning. Emphasize the value of acquiring new knowledge and skills, and remain open to feedback and constructive criticism.

3. **Engage in Self-Evaluation:** Develop metacognitive skills by critically evaluating your own performance. Regularly assess your strengths and weaknesses, and compare your self-perception with objective measures to gain a more accurate understanding of your competence.

4. **Embrace Expertise:** Acknowledge and appreciate the expertise of others. Collaborate with knowledgeable individuals, seek their advice, and recognize that their insights can contribute to better decision-making and personal growth.

5. **Foster a Culture of Feedback:** Encourage a feedback-rich environment in professional and personal settings. Promote open communication, constructive criticism, and peer evaluation, creating opportunities for individuals to receive honest assessments of their abilities.

Words of Wisdom: The secret to happiness is freedom. The secret of freedom is courage.

– Thucydides

Chapter 20
Boiling Frog Syndrome

The boiling frog syndrome is a cautionary tale about the risks of progressive adaptation to adversity. To avoid being a victim of this phenomenon, it is critical to build awareness and attentiveness. In this chapter, we will look at numerous awareness techniques that can assist us in staying attentive, recognizing symptoms of deterioration, and taking proactive measures toward positive change. By recognizing the signs of the boiling frog syndrome relationships, you can actively work towards maintaining healthy connections and preventing the irreversible damage that may occur if left unattended. Similar to the boiling frog syndrome story, relationships can sometimes experience a gradual deterioration that goes unnoticed until it reaches a critical point.

Boiling Frog Syndrome

Frogs hopped and basked in the warm sun in a quiet town near a pond. Unbeknownst to them, an experiment known as the "Boiling Frog Syndrome" was in the works. A cunning human placed a saucepan on a stove near the pond, gradually heating the water. The frogs were oblivious to the danger as the temperature climbed slowly. They grew acclimated to the warmth, ignorant that it was growing dangerous. The frogs were unable to flee because they failed to recognize the small shift. The water eventually boiled over, trapping and killing them as a result of their incapacity to recognise incremental adjustments.

7 Solutions to Avoid Boiling Frog Syndrome

1. Education and information:

Knowledge is a potent weapon in the fight against the boiling frog syndrome psychology. Actively seeking knowledge and educating oneself on important matters allows us to make educated decisions. We must constantly learn to broaden our understanding, whether it be about environmental concerns, social inequities, or personal well-being.

2. Vital Thinking:

It is vital to develop critical thinking skills in order to avoid complacency. We must question assumptions, challenge dominant narratives, and do essential information analysis. By exploring diverse points of view, we can avoid accepting the status quo and get a better knowledge of complex topics.

3. Mindfulness and Self-Reflection:

Practicing mindfulness and self-reflection assists us to become more aware of our emotions, thoughts, and experiences. Taking the time to consider our beliefs, objectives, and the consequences of our actions allows us to stay connected to our true selves. Mindfulness also allows us to detect minor changes in our surroundings and relationships, which prevents us from progressively adapting to adverse conditions.

4. Dialogue and Debate:

Engaging in meaningful talks and arguments with people creates a greater awareness of various points of view. We get insights that challenge our prejudices by actively listening and exchanging ideas. Constructive discussion can also be used to raise communal consciousness by providing spaces for shared learning and action.

5. Seeking Diverse Sources of Information:

It is critical to seek out diverse sources of information in order to avoid becoming imprisoned in an echo chamber and consuming a diverse range of viewpoints, especially those that disagree with our own, which aids in the development of a more thorough knowledge of the world. This variety of input keeps us from becoming oblivious to bad changes or contemptuous of opposing opinions.

6. Building Supportive Networks:

Surrounding ourselves with like-minded people who share our beliefs and objectives is beneficial. Participating in communities, organizations, or social networks that actively advocate good change fosters a sense of shared duty and accountability. These networks serve as reminders to be aware and to act when necessary.

7. Setting Goals and Regular Evaluation:

Setting personal objectives that are connected with our beliefs and constantly monitoring our progress is an excellent method to keep us engaged and prevent complacency. We can discover any subtle adjustments that may require our attention by occasionally reassessing our behaviors and outcomes. This procedure also assists us in remaining motivated and committed to ongoing progress.

Words of Wisdom: The greatest danger for most of us is not that our aim is too high and we miss it, but that it is too low and we reach it.

– Michelangelo

Chapter 21

Eye-Opening Psychological Truths

In our quest for a fulfilling and balanced life, understanding some fundamental psychological truths can offer valuable insights and strategies for improving our well-being. Here are six eye-opening psychological truths that can transform the way we navigate our personal and professional relationships, manage our emotions, and ultimately lead a more satisfying life.

1. Don't Overshare: Privacy Is Power

In an age where social media and constant connectivity have become the norm, it's tempting to share every detail of our lives. However, oversharing can lead to unintended consequences. Privacy is not just a right but a powerful tool in maintaining control over our personal information. When we share too much, we expose ourselves to judgment, misinterpretation, and potential manipulation.

The key psychological insight is both straightforward and deep: individuals can't undermine what they're unaware of. By keeping certain aspects of our lives private, we protect ourselves from unnecessary vulnerability and maintain a sense of control over our personal narrative. This approach allows us to build trust gradually, ensuring that our relationships are based on mutual respect and understanding rather than on the superficial knowledge shared online.

2. Don't Take Everything Personally

It's common to believe that the way others act or speak is a reflection of us, which can lead to undue stress and self-doubt. However, the reality is that people are generally preoccupied with their own lives, worries, and insecurities, meaning their behavior is more about their own issues than about you. Recognizing this fact can free us from the habit of taking things personally. By understanding that others' actions and remarks stem from their own experiences and struggles, we can keep a more balanced perspective and prevent their behavior from impacting our self-esteem and emotional health.

3. Focus on Solutions, Not Problems

It's common to find ourselves dwelling on problems, which can lead to feelings of helplessness and frustration. However, the psychological truth is that focusing on problems often exacerbates them, making them appear larger and more insurmountable. Conversely, when we shift our focus to finding solutions, we open ourselves up to opportunities and potential resolutions.

By adopting a solution-oriented mindset, we train our brains to seek out positive actions and constructive strategies. This shift not only helps us overcome obstacles more effectively but also fosters a proactive approach to challenges, ultimately leading to a more optimistic and empowered outlook on life.

4. Those Who Share Gossip with You Are Likely to Share Gossip About You

Gossip can be enticing, offering a sense of connection or superiority, but it's important to recognize its double-edged nature. The psychological truth here is that individuals who engage in gossip about others are likely to gossip about you as well. When someone shares private information or talks negatively about others, it's often a sign of their own insecurities or a need for validation.

Understanding this can help us navigate our social circles more wisely. It's crucial to build relationships based on trust and respect rather than engaging in or endorsing gossip. This approach fosters healthier, more supportive interactions and protects our own reputation and relationships.

5. Lack of Communication Can Kill a Great Relationship

Clear and open communication is essential for the success of any relationship, be it personal or professional. The psychological truth here is that a lack of communication can lead to misunderstandings, unresolved conflicts, and emotional distance. When we fail to express our needs, concerns, and feelings, we create a void that can be filled with assumptions and misinterpretations.

Investing in open, honest, and empathetic communication helps build stronger connections and resolves potential issues before they escalate. By actively listening and sharing our thoughts and emotions, we contribute to a more transparent and supportive relationship, fostering mutual understanding and trust.

6. Caring Less Can Lead to Greater Happiness

In a world where external opinions and societal expectations often dictate our actions and feelings, learning to detach ourselves from what others think can be liberating. The psychological truth is that the less we care about others' judgments and the more we focus on our own values and happiness, the more content and at peace we become.

By prioritizing our own well-being and aligning our actions with our personal values, we free ourselves from the burden of seeking validation from others. This shift in focus allows us to cultivate genuine self-acceptance and inner satisfaction, leading to a more joyful and fulfilling life.

Words of Wisdom: I have learned silence from the talkative, toleration from the intolerant, and kindness from the unkind.

– Khalil Gibran

Chapter 22

SISU: The Finnish Concept of Resilience

In a world filled with challenges and setbacks, the quest for resilience has become paramount. Resilience is more than just overcoming hardship; it's about flourishing in the midst of it. And when it comes to resilience, few cultures embody it as profoundly as the Finns, who have a word for this indomitable spirit: Sisu.

Sisu, pronounced "see-soo," is a unique Finnish concept that encapsulates grit, determination, and courage in the face of adversity. It's an intrinsic quality deeply embedded in the Finnish psyche, influencing how they approach life's challenges. But what exactly is Sisu, and how can we incorporate this powerful mindset into our own lives?

At its core, Sisu is about perseverance in the face of extreme adversity. It's the ability to summon inner strength and tenacity when confronted with seemingly insurmountable obstacles. While resilience is a universal trait found in every culture, Sisu has distinct characteristics that set it apart.

SISU: The Finnish Concept of Resilience

First and foremost, Sisu is about having the courage to take action, even when the odds are stacked against you. It's the willingness to confront adversity head-on and push through despite the discomfort or fear. For the Finns, Sisu is not just about enduring hardships passively but actively engaging with them, facing challenges with unwavering determination.

One of the defining features of Sisu is its emphasis on perseverance over perfection. It's about embracing the journey rather than fixating solely on the outcome. Finnish culture celebrates the process of overcoming obstacles, recognizing that growth often occurs through struggle and adversity.

Furthermore, Sisu is rooted in a deep sense of self-belief and confidence. It's about trusting in your abilities and having faith that you can overcome whatever obstacles come your way. This unwavering self-assurance empowers individuals to push beyond their limits and achieve feats they once thought impossible.

But perhaps the most remarkable aspect of Sisu is its collective nature. While it is often portrayed as an individual trait, Sisu also encompasses a sense of community and solidarity. In Finland, there's a cultural expectation to support one another during challenging times, fostering a collective resilience that strengthens the entire society.

So, how can we cultivate Sisu in our own lives? While it may seem like an innate quality reserved for the Finns, Sisu is a mindset that can be developed and nurtured over time.

Firstly, it's essential to embrace discomfort and adversity rather than shying away from them. Instead of viewing challenges as obstacles to be avoided, see them as opportunities for growth and self-improvement. Adopting a growth mindset allows you to approach setbacks with resilience and determination, knowing that you have the capacity to overcome them.

Secondly, cultivate a strong sense of purpose and passion in everything you do. Having a clear vision of what you want to achieve provides the motivation and drive to persevere in the face of adversity. Whether it's pursuing a personal goal or striving for societal change, anchoring yourself in a sense of purpose fuels your resilience and determination.

Additionally, practice self-compassion and self-care as you navigate life's challenges. Resilience isn't about constantly pushing yourself to the brink; it's about knowing when to rest and recharge. Prioritize your well-being and cultivate habits that promote physical, emotional, and mental health.

Finally, foster connections and support networks within your community. Just as the Finns rely on each other for strength during difficult times, surround yourself with people who uplift and encourage you. Building a strong support system provides the foundation for resilience, knowing that you're not alone in facing life's challenges.

Words of Wisdom: Every champion was once a contender who refused to give up.

– **Rocky Balboa**

Chapter 23

Aristotle's Four Causes: The Why

The renowned Greek philosopher Aristotle made significant contributions to various fields of knowledge, including metaphysics, ethics, and natural sciences. Among his notable concepts, Aristotle introduced the theory of the Four Causes, which seeks to explain the essence of existence. These four causes delve into the underlying reasons and principles that govern the nature of things.

1. The Material Cause:

The material cause refers to the substance or matter from which something is made. According to Aristotle, everything in the world is composed of matter, and this matter is a fundamental component in understanding the nature of an object. For example, the material cause of a statue could be the marble from which it is sculpted. By identifying the material cause, we gain insights into an object's physical properties and characteristics.

2. The Formal Cause:

The formal cause represents the form or structure that gives an object its particular shape or identity. It is the essence or blueprint that defines what an object is. For instance, in the case of a statue, the formal cause would be the idea or concept that the sculptor had in mind while creating it. The formal cause provides the organizing principle that shapes the matter and gives it a distinct identity.

3. The Efficient Cause:

The efficient cause deals with the agent or force that brings about the change or creation of an object. It refers to the action or process that sets things in motion. In the example of a statue, the efficient cause would be the sculptor's skill and craftsmanship, as well as the tools and techniques used to shape the marble. The efficient cause is responsible for the transformation from potentiality to actuality, bringing the object into existence.

4. The Final Cause:

The final cause Aristotle focuses on the ultimate purpose or goal for which something exists. It explores the reason or intention behind an object's creation or existence. In the case of a statue, the final cause could be aesthetic appreciation, religious devotion, or commemoration. The final cause gives meaning and direction to the object, guiding its purpose and defining its significance.

Significance of Aristotle's Four Causes

1. **Comprehensive Understanding:** The Four Causes provide a comprehensive framework for understanding the nature and essence of things. By considering the material, formal, efficient, and final causes, we gain a holistic perspective on the object and its place in the world.

2. **Causal Analysis:** The Four Causes encourage critical thinking and analysis by prompting us to consider different aspects of causality. This approach helps us go beyond surface-level observations and delve deeper into the underlying principles at work.

3. **Teleological Perspective:** Aristotle's emphasis on the final cause introduces a teleological perspective, highlighting the importance of purpose and goal-oriented behaviour. It reminds us that everything in the natural world has a purpose or end to which it aspires.

4. **Application in Various Fields:** The Four Causes have influenced numerous disciplines, including philosophy, science, art, and ethics. They offer a versatile framework that can be applied to understanding phenomena and explaining the relationships between cause and effect.

Words of Wisdom: Wisdom cannot come by railroad or automobile or aeroplane, or be hurried up by telegraph or telephone.

– Henry Ford

Chapter 24

Delboeuf Illusion: Why you eat too much

Have you ever wondered why you might be consuming more food than you actually need? The answer may lie in a fascinating psychological phenomenon known as the Delboeuf Illusion.

Understanding the Delboeuf Illusion:

The Delboeuf Illusion psychology concept revolves around the perception of size and the impact it has on our judgments. Named after the Belgian psychologist Joseph Remi Leopold Delboeuf, this optical illusion manifests when we misjudge the size of objects, particularly when they are surrounded by a larger or smaller context.

How does it relate to eating habits?

When it comes to our plates and portion sizes, the Delboeuf Illusion can significantly influence our perception. Imagine a scenario where you are presented with a smaller portion on a large plate versus the same portion on a smaller plate. The illusion tricks our minds into thinking that the larger plate holds a smaller amount of food, leading us to subconsciously believe that we need more to feel satisfied.

Examples of the Delboeuf Illusion in Action:

To illustrate this phenomenon with concrete Delboeuf illusion examples, let's consider a classic case. Picture a dinner plate with a standard serving of spaghetti. Place this plate on a larger platter, and suddenly, the spaghetti appears minuscule. Now, transfer the same serving to a smaller plate, and voila! The portion looks more substantial.

Restaurants often strategically leverage the Delboeuf Illusion to influence customer behavior. By serving meals on larger plates, they create an optical illusion that encourages patrons to perceive their portions as smaller, prompting them to order more food. This subtle manipulation of visual cues highlights how the Delboeuf Illusion can play a role not only in our perception of portion sizes at home but also in shaping our choices when dining out.

How the Delboeuf Illusion Affects Overeating:

The implications of the Delboeuf Illusion on our eating habits are profound. Studies suggest that individuals are more likely to overeat when faced with larger plates, as the illusion tricks them into believing they need larger portions to satisfy their hunger.

Moreover, the illusion extends beyond plate size. Consider the role of serving bowls and glasses in influencing our consumption. A bowl filled halfway may seem emptier on a larger table, leading us to ladle on more than we actually need. Similarly, a tall glass can make a standard beverage appear smaller, potentially prompting us to pour ourselves another serving.

Practical Tips to Counteract the Delboeuf Illusion:

Now that we understand the impact of the Delboeuf Illusion on our eating behavior, let's explore practical strategies to counteract its effects:

1. **Mindful Plating:** Be conscious of portion sizes and choose smaller plates when serving meals. This simple adjustment can help align your perception with the actual quantity of food you need.

2. **Awareness in Restaurants:** When dining out, pay attention to plate sizes. If you notice that a restaurant tends to use larger plates, consider sharing a dish or ordering a smaller portion to avoid overeating.

3. **Use Visual Cues:** Instead of relying solely on plate size, pay attention to visual cues that indicate portion sizes. This includes using measuring tools or familiar objects to gauge appropriate serving sizes.

Words of Wisdom: Look well to this one day, for it and it alone is life. In the brief course of this day lie all the verities and realities of your existence.

– Kalidasa

Chapter 25

The Law of Attraction vs. The Law of Vibration

In the realm of self-help and personal development, two powerful concepts often take center stage: The Law of Attraction and The Law of Vibration. While these principles share common ground in their pursuit of understanding the universe's intricacies, they also exhibit distinct characteristics that set them apart. In this exploration, we'll delve into the core of The Law of Attraction and The Law of Vibration, uncovering their nuances and deciphering how they influence our daily lives.

The Law of Attraction

The Law of Attraction gained widespread popularity with the release of Rhonda Byrne's "The Secret." At its essence, this law posits that like attracts like—our thoughts and feelings shape our reality, drawing similar energies and experiences into our lives. The underlying belief is that by maintaining positive thoughts and emotions, we can manifest our desires and create a more fulfilling existence.

Proponents of The Law of Attraction advocate for the power of visualization, positive affirmations, and maintaining an optimistic mindset. The idea is to align one's thoughts and emotions with the desired outcome, sending a signal to the universe that attracts corresponding energy.

Critics argue that The Law of Attraction oversimplifies the complexities of life, attributing success solely to positive thinking. While cultivating a positive mindset is undoubtedly beneficial, some believe that neglecting practical actions and hard work may lead to unfulfilled aspirations.

The Law of Vibration

On the other hand, The Law of Vibration operates on the premise that everything in the universe vibrates at a specific frequency. This includes thoughts, emotions, and even inanimate objects. According to this law, aligning oneself with the right frequencies can influence the outcomes and experiences in one's life.

In contrast to The Law of Attraction's emphasis on thoughts and emotions, The Law of Vibration highlights the importance of energetic frequencies. Advocates of this law suggest that by raising one's vibrational frequency through positive emotions, gratitude, and mindfulness, individuals can attract corresponding energies and experiences.

Connecting the Dots

While The Law of Attraction and The Law of Vibration may appear distinct, they are intricately connected. The vibrations we emit through our thoughts and emotions are believed to be the magnetic force that draws similar energies into our lives. In essence, The Law of Attraction can be seen as a manifestation of The Law of Vibration.

To illustrate this connection, imagine yourself as a tuning fork. The vibrations you emit resonate with energies of similar frequencies in the universe. If your internal tuning is set to positivity, gratitude, and abundance, you are more likely to attract experiences and opportunities vibrating at the same frequency.

Practical Applications

Both laws offer practical applications for those seeking to enhance their lives. Combining the power of positive thinking from The Law of Attraction with the vibrational alignment suggested by The Law of Vibration creates a holistic approach to personal development.

1. **Mindfulness Practices:** Engage in mindfulness practices such as meditation and deep breathing to raise your vibrational frequency. This not only enhances your overall well-being but also aligns your thoughts and emotions with positive outcomes.

2. **Visualization and Affirmations:** Use visualization and positive affirmations to harness The Law of Attraction. Envision your goals with clarity and affirm them regularly, reinforcing the positive energy you wish to attract.

3. **Gratitude Journaling:** Cultivate an attitude of gratitude to elevate your vibrational frequency. Regularly journaling about the things you are thankful for creates a positive energetic shift.

Words of Wisdom: You can't be hurt when you know that you are the master of your thoughts, reactions, and emotions.

– Wayne Dyer

Chapter 26

Manifest Anything With the 3–6–9 Manifestation Method

The 3–6–9 approach has drawn a lot of interest in the field of manifestation methods because of its apparent efficacy and ease of use. This method, attributed to the legendary inventor and visionary Nikola Tesla, is believed to tap into the universal energy to manifest desires.

Understanding the 3-6–9 Manifestation Method

Step 1: Choose Your Affirmation

The initial phase of the 3–6–9 manifestation method involves picking a clear and precise affirmation that represents your desired outcome. This affirmation should be positive, specific, and resonate with your true intentions. It serves as the focal point for your manifestation efforts.

Step 2: Repetition in Sets of 3

Begin by repeating your chosen affirmation three times in the morning. This sets the intention for the day ahead. Follow it up with another set of three repetitions during the afternoon. Finally, before bedtime, repeat the affirmation three more times. The repetition in sets of three is believed to align with the universal energy and reinforce the manifestation process.

Step 3: Expand to Sets of 6

After several days of practicing the 3-repetition cycle, progress to sets of six. Recite your affirmation six times during the morning, afternoon, and evening. This stage is considered a crucial expansion, intensifying the manifestation energy and strengthening the connection between your intention and the universe.

Step 4: Amplify with Sets of 9

The final step involves repeating your affirmation in sets of nine. This amplification is the culmination of the 3–6–9 manifestation method. Perform three sets of nine repetitions—morning, afternoon, and evening. This step is considered the peak of the manifestation process, where the energy is believed to reach its zenith, aligning the universe with your desires.

Unveiling the Power Behind 3-6-9

Numerological Significance:

The 3–6–9 manifestation method draws inspiration from the numerological significance of these numbers. Nikola Tesla famously stated, "If you only knew the magnificence of the 3, 6, and 9, then you would have the key to the universe." While the mystical nature of this statement may be open to interpretation, adherents of the method believe that these numbers hold a unique vibrational frequency that resonates with the manifestation process.

Quantum Physics Connection:

Proponents of the 3–6–9 method often draw connections to quantum physics principles. Tesla himself was deeply involved in groundbreaking work in this field. The method is thought to tap into the quantum field, leveraging the power of intention and energy to influence reality.

Addressing Common Concerns

What if You Miss a Day of 369 Manifestation?

Consistency is key in manifestation practices, but missing a day is not necessarily a cause for concern. The 3–6–9 method emphasizes the overall dedication to the process rather than fixating on individual days. If a day is missed, some practitioners recommend doubling the repetitions on the following day to maintain the momentum. The key is to cultivate a positive and focused mindset throughout the manifestation journey.

Words of Wisdom: Keep going, because every step forward brings you one step closer to your goals.

– Brian Tracy

Chapter 27

30-Day Plan for a Flat Belly and Better Health

Belly fat goes beyond being a mere cosmetic issue; it is a serious health hazard. Known as visceral fat, it surrounds vital organs and elevates the risk of heart disease, type 2 diabetes, and even certain cancers. Having excess belly fat can significantly raise your risk of a heart attack. If you're committed to improving your health, targeting belly fat is essential.

1. Regular Physical Activity:

Engaging in regular exercise is crucial for burning fat and building muscle, both vital for achieving a flatter belly. Cardiovascular workouts are beneficial, but combining them with strength training is particularly effective for reducing belly fat and improving overall fitness.

The Impact of Regular Exercise:

- **Strength Training 3-5 Times a Week:** Lifting weights builds muscle and boosts your resting metabolic rate, allowing you to burn more calories even when at rest.

- **Strength Training vs. Cardio:** Cardio exercises burn calories during the workout, but strength training continues to burn calories after exercising due to the muscle repair process.

- **Walking 10,000-20,000 Steps Daily:** Simple yet effective, walking helps burn calories and reduce belly fat. 10,000 steps a day can maximize health benefits.

- **Embrace Muscle Soreness:** Muscle soreness after a workout indicates that your muscles are repairing and growing, which enhances fat burning through increased growth hormone levels.

2. Opt for Nutrient-Dense Foods

Reducing belly fat involves more than just calorie cutting; it requires making informed food choices. Nutrient-dense foods supply essential vitamins, minerals, and amino acids that support metabolism, increase energy, and promote fat burning.

Benefits of Choosing Nutrient-Dense Foods:

- **Sustained Energy Levels:** Foods like leafy greens, lean proteins, and whole grains provide continuous energy, keeping you active throughout the day without constant snacking.

- **Boosted Metabolism:** Nutrient-rich foods support metabolic processes, helping your body burn fat more efficiently, even when inactive.

- **Disease Prevention:** A diet rich in nutrient-dense foods lowers the risk of chronic conditions such as obesity, heart disease, and diabetes, which are linked to excess belly fat.

Incorporate lean proteins, vegetables, fruits, nuts, seeds, and whole grains into your meals to ensure a broad range of nutrients that aid in weight loss and overall health improvement.

3. Stay Hydrated

Proper hydration is often underestimated in weight loss, yet it's essential for achieving a flat belly and maintaining health. Water aids in regulating metabolism, improving skin health, and controlling unnecessary cravings.

Why Staying Hydrated Matters:

- **Skin Health:** Proper hydration helps keep your skin smooth and clear by flushing out toxins.

- **Youthful Appearance:** Drinking enough water maintains skin elasticity, reducing the appearance of fine lines and wrinkles.

- **Enhanced Metabolism:** Adequate hydration improves your body's ability to metabolize fat, supporting weight loss.

- **Reduced Cravings:** Dehydration is frequently mistaken for hunger, leading to unnecessary snacking. Staying hydrated helps prevent these cravings.

Try to consume 2-4 liters of water each day, adjusting based on your activity level and environment. If you are physically active or live in a hotter climate, you may need to increase your water intake.

4. Prioritize Quality Sleep

Adequate sleep is crucial for an effective weight loss plan. It is crucial in hormone regulation, muscle recovery, and overall health. Poor sleep can elevate cortisol levels, a stress hormone that promotes belly fat storage.

Strategies for Better Sleep:

- **Invest in Comfortable Bedding:** A high-quality mattress and pillows provide necessary support and improve sleep quality.

- **Create a Dark Sleep Environment:** Ensure your bedroom is completely dark to avoid disrupting your circadian rhythm, leading to deeper sleep.

- **Align with Natural Sleep Cycles:** Going to bed early, ideally by 9:00-10:00 PM, helps align your body with its natural rhythms for more restorative sleep.

- **Keep Your Room Cool**: A temperature of 17-20°C is ideal for sleep, mimicking the natural drop in body temperature that occurs at night, aiding in faster and deeper sleep.

Implement the 3-2-1 Sleep Rule:

- **Avoid Eating 3 Hours Before Bed:** Late eating can disrupt sleep and hinder fat-burning processes. No meals 3 hours before sleeping

- **Reduce Fluids 2 Hours Before Bed:** Cut back on fluids two hours before bedtime to prevent nighttime bathroom trips.

- **No Screens 1 Hour Before Bed**: Blue light from screens interferes with melatonin production, which regulates sleep. Shut all your screens one hour before bed.

5. **Manage Stress and Surround Yourself with Positivity**

Effective stress management is essential for reducing belly fat. Elevated stress levels boost cortisol, a hormone that encourages fat accumulation, especially in the abdominal area. Managing stress and surrounding yourself with positive influences can help you stay on track with your fitness goals.

Choose Your Social Circle Wisely:

- **Spend Time with Active People:** Being around individuals who prioritize fitness can motivate you to stay active and committed to your goals.

- **Eat Healthily Together:** Friends who value healthy eating can support you in making better food choices and sticking to your diet.

- **Stay Positive with Open-Minded Friends**: Surrounding yourself with positive, open-minded people can help maintain a good attitude, even during challenges.

- **Embrace Accountability:** Friends who hold you accountable can encourage you to stay focused on your fitness goals.

Understanding Cortisol and Its Role:

Cortisol is essential for managing stress but high levels can lead to increased belly fat. Managing stress effectively is key to reducing belly fat and improving overall health.

Words of Wisdom: The idea is to die young as late as possible.

– Ashley Montagu

Section 4

Life Lessons and Timeless Truths

There was a giant mango tree near our home, its branches sprawling wide and tall, providing shade to the nearby street and bearing fruit every summer. It was a tree that we all admired, its sturdy trunk and lush green canopy a symbol of resilience. For years, the tree had stood tall through the seasons, its roots deep and hidden beneath the earth, unseen by most. As a child, I would often sit beneath its shade, reading books or simply enjoying the cool breeze that swayed its leaves. The tree was a quiet companion in my daily life, its presence a source of comfort.

One year, a fierce storm rolled in, with winds so strong that they rattled windows and bent the tallest of branches. The rain came in torrents, flooding the streets and drenching everything in sight. I remember watching from the window as the tree, usually so steadfast, began to sway under the storm's relentless force. The storm lasted through the night, and by morning, the scene outside was transformed. The mango tree that had stood so proudly for decades had fallen. Its great trunk lay across the ground, its once-strong branches scattered, and its roots were exposed, twisted and sprawling out from the earth like the arms of a giant.

I stood there for what felt like hours, staring at the tree in awe. It was no longer the symbol of strength I had always seen it as. It was a victim of nature's power, seemingly defeated. But as I looked closer at the exposed roots, something struck me. Beneath the earth, hidden from view, there had been a network of roots intertwining, supporting one another, each one working in unison to hold the tree in place. Despite the storm's fury, the tree had stood for so long because of this intricate system of support beneath the surface. The wind had uprooted it, but those roots had quietly provided it with the strength to grow tall in the first place.

This revelation stayed with me, and I couldn't help but reflect on how it mirrored the way we approach life. Often, we see people's success, their outward achievements, the fruits they bear, but we don't see the unseen efforts that hold them up—the quiet work that goes on beneath the surface. Just like the mango tree, we need to build strong foundations, cultivate the roots of our character and resilience, so that we can withstand the storms of life.

In the years that followed, I realized that life isn't just about the visible fruits of success—it's about the invisible principles and lessons that shape our growth. The tree's fall taught me that the things we cannot see—the lessons we learn, the values we hold, the time we invest—are often the most important.

Through this experience, I also began to notice the paradoxes that life presents. We live in a world where we are constantly told to control everything, to manage every detail. But the truth I came to learn was that control is often an illusion. The more we try to control everything, the more we become slaves to our own expectations. The paradox of control is that true power lies in letting go. It's about understanding that not everything can be managed, and sometimes, the most powerful thing we can do is to surrender and trust the process.

As I continued to grow, I found myself using these principles as guides for navigating life. The lessons from the fallen mango tree, the roots beneath the surface, became the foundation for my approach to living a fulfilled and purposeful life. I started to pay attention to the things that really mattered—the values, the relationships, and the moments that made life meaningful.

The storm that uprooted the mango tree did not defeat it—it merely revealed the underlying strength that had always been there. In the same way, life's challenges and hardships do not define us, but they reveal who we truly are. The deeper we dig, the stronger our foundations become, and the more we are able to thrive, not despite the storms, but because of them.

Chapter 28

Effective Exercises to Boost Your Confidence

Confidence grows gradually through consistent practice of self-assurance techniques. One of the best ways to nurture confidence is by engaging in specific exercises that help refine your communication skills and self-presentation. Here are four practical exercises designed to boost your confidence, improve your communication, and help you feel more comfortable in various social and professional settings.

1. Mirror Practice: Improve Your Self-Image

A great way to develop confidence is by practicing in front of a mirror. Stand in front of a mirror and deliver a short speech or presentation, focusing on your body language, tone of voice, and facial expressions. Pay attention to how you present yourself, adjust your posture, maintain eye contact, and refine your gestures. Imagine yourself speaking with authority and purpose as you deliver your message. This exercise helps you gain a better understanding of how others see you, which is a powerful way to enhance self-confidence. By observing yourself, you can identify areas for improvement and get comfortable with your unique style. Over time, you'll notice an improvement in both your self-assurance and your overall presentation skills.

2. Role-Playing to Enhance Communication Skills

Role-playing is an excellent exercise for building confidence, especially in scenarios where effective communication is essential. Enlist the help of a friend, colleague, or family member, and take turns role-playing different types of conversations. You could practice delivering feedback, expressing opinions, or handling difficult discussions. By switching between roles and experimenting with different communication styles, you can learn how to handle various situations with ease. Role-playing allows you to prepare for real-life interactions by practicing how you react, respond, and communicate. It's also a great way to receive constructive feedback on your communication skills, which can ultimately help you improve and feel more at ease in similar situations.

3. Daily Positive Affirmations

Positive affirmations are a powerful way to cultivate inner confidence. Begin by drafting a list of affirmations that capture the confidence and clarity you want to embrace. For example, you could include statements like, "I am a clear and powerful communicator" or "I speak with confidence and assurance." Repeat these affirmations every day, especially before important conversations, presentations, or meetings. Positive affirmations help shift your mindset, enabling you to overcome self-doubt and approach situations with a more positive outlook. When you repeat them consistently, affirmations can gradually change your self-perception, allowing you to internalize a more confident self-image.

4. Challenge Yourself to Speak Up

Regularly stepping outside your comfort zone is one of the most effective methods for enhancing your confidence. Actively seek opportunities to voice your thoughts in group settings, ask questions, or participate in discussions. Start with small group meetings, then work your way up to larger audiences. By pushing yourself to contribute, you'll become more accustomed to expressing your ideas and engaging with others, which can significantly reduce anxiety and boost self-confidence. Additionally, frequent participation helps you develop resilience to social pressure, enhancing your ability to speak confidently and connect with people. Each time you rise to these challenges, you reinforce your confidence and refine your communication skills, making future interactions feel much easier.

Words of Wisdom: Confidence is a skill built through small, consistent actions. It's not about being perfect but embracing growth, stepping out of your comfort zone, and believing in your potential. Practice, persistence, and self-compassion are the keys to unlocking your best self.

– Dr. Michelle Harper

Chapter 29

Regrets You'll Wish You Had Avoided

Life is a journey full of opportunities to grow, connect, and create lasting memories. However, along the way, many find themselves looking back with regret, often because of choices they made or actions they didn't take. By being mindful of some common regrets, you can make more intentional choices that align with a fulfilling and meaningful life. Here are five regrets you may want to avoid:

1. Letting the Opinions of Others Limit Your Potential

Many people let others' opinions dictate their choices, avoiding opportunities or dreams simply because someone else expressed doubt or negativity. When you allow someone else's judgment to overshadow your goals, your potential remains untapped, and your passions remain unexplored. Remember that each person's journey is unique, and what works for one may not be the path for another. Embrace your ambitions, and allow your talents to flourish without the constraints of others' opinions. This mindset can prevent the regret of realizing later in life that you let the fears or doubts of others hold you back.

2. Dwelling on the Past Instead of Embracing the Present

While reflection can be helpful, living in the past often brings more harm than good. Many people regret spending so much time rethinking past choices, conversations, and decisions, rather than focusing on what's happening right now. Dwelling on past mistakes or missed opportunities keeps you from being present and limits your enjoyment of life as it unfolds. Embracing each day as it comes helps you build a life with fewer regrets because you're making the most of every moment, creating memories, and truly living rather than just reflecting.

3. Investing Time in People Who Don't Value Your Growth

Time is one of the most valuable things you can give, so it's worth sharing it with people who truly support and care about your well-being. Unfortunately, many find themselves regretting the years spent around individuals who didn't have their best interests at heart. These relationships can drain your energy, self-confidence, and passion. Instead, invest your time in friendships and connections that lift you up, encourage your goals, and respect your boundaries. By surrounding yourself with people who want the best for you, you create a supportive network that contributes to your happiness and success.

4. Overlooking the Importance of Family

In the rush of daily life, family can sometimes take a back seat to careers, hobbies, or social pursuits. However, family relationships often hold a unique and irreplaceable significance, offering unconditional love and support through life's highs and lows. Many people regret not prioritizing their family, only realizing this after losing time or missing out on important moments. Whether it's sharing quality time, expressing appreciation, or just being there when needed, making family a priority is a decision you won't regret. Relationships with family are among the most enduring, and nurturing these bonds brings a sense of joy, connection, and fulfillment.

5. Avoiding Risks and Staying in the Comfort Zone

Taking risks often means venturing into uncharted territory, which can be intimidating. Yet, steering clear of risks altogether may result in a life filled with "what could have been" and lost chances. Many people look back on their lives wishing they had taken more chances, whether in their careers, relationships, or personal growth. Playing it safe may seem appealing, but it often leads to a limited experience of life. Embracing reasonable risks can open doors to growth, learning, and achievements that would have been impossible otherwise. By daring to take that leap, you're creating a life full of experiences, lessons, and potential successes, rather than living with regrets of untapped possibilities.

Words of Wisdom: Regret often stems not from what we did, but from what we chose not to do. Life rewards courage, curiosity, and connection—so dare to dream, act, and love boldly. Avoid the shadows of missed opportunities by living with intention and heart.

– Eleanor Parker

Chapter 30

7 Effective Strategies to Soothe Yourself When Life Gets Tough

Life can often feel overwhelming, and during challenging times, it's easy to feel lost or anxious. However, there are several strategies you can use to soothe yourself and regain a sense of control. Here are seven effective ways to help you navigate through difficult moments.

1. Take a Walk: Clear Your Head and Shift Your Perspective

When life becomes too much to handle, sometimes the best remedy is to take a walk. Walking allows you to physically distance yourself from the source of stress, providing both your body and mind with a much-needed break. The rhythmic motion of walking can help reduce tension, elevate your mood, and clear your thoughts. This mindful focus can help ground you in the present moment, offering a fresh perspective on the challenges you're facing. Often, taking a step back—even for a short walk—can help you return to the situation with a clearer and more positive mindset.

2. Treat Yourself to a Day of Self-Care: Recharge and Refresh

In the hustle and bustle of daily life, it's common to neglect the significance of self-care. Taking a day to engage in activities that bring you joy and relaxation can be incredibly refreshing. Whether it's reading a book, watching your favorite shows, taking a long bath, or simply enjoying a quiet moment, giving yourself this time is crucial. This day isn't about accomplishing tasks or being productive; it's about recharging your mental and emotional energy.

3. Practice Acts of Kindness: The Uplifting Power of Giving

Whether it's offering your time, a kind word, or a small gift to a stranger, giving can create a warm and uplifting feeling within you. Generosity also shifts your focus from your own struggles to the needs of others, providing a sense of purpose and connection. This simple act of kindness can remind you that even during difficult times, you have the power to make a positive difference in someone else's life.

4. Embrace the Journey: Understand That Challenges Are Temporary

When you're facing difficulties, it's important to remember that life is a journey. The situation you're facing is only temporary, and it won't last forever. Every challenge you overcome adds to your resilience and strength, equipping you to handle future obstacles with greater ease. By maintaining a wider perspective and recognizing that difficult times are merely a part of your journey, you can discover the resilience to continue moving forward.

5. Let the Tears Flow: Release Your Emotions

Crying is frequently mistaken for weakness, but it's a natural and beneficial way to release accumulated emotions. When you're feeling overwhelmed, allowing yourself to cry can offer a significant emotional release, helping you to feel more at peace.

Crying serves as an emotional outlet that helps you process what you're going through. It can also be a cathartic experience, enabling you to let go of some of the stress and tension you've been holding onto. After a good cry, many people feel a sense of relief, as if a weight has been lifted off their shoulders.

6. Rediscover Your Inner Child: Lighten Up and Have Fun

In the midst of life's challenges, it's easy to become overly serious and forget the importance of having fun. Being playful helps you tap into the carefree spirit you had as a child, reminding you that not everything needs to be taken so seriously.

7. Reflect on Your Strengths: Boost Your Confidence and Resilience

When times get challenging, it's natural to dwell on the negatives. Take a moment to write down a list of 20 qualities, skills, and abilities that make you who you are. Focusing on your strengths can enhance your confidence and remind you that you have the resources within you to overcome challenges. This exercise can also help you shift from a mindset of defeat to one of empowerment, reinforcing your resilience and capability.

Words of Wisdom: Thank yourself for how far you've come. It hasn't been easy.

– Ralph Smart

Chapter 31

10 Uncomfortable Truths about Life: Facing the Hard Reality

Life is a multifaceted voyage encompassing peaks and valleys, moments of happiness, and moments of sadness. Acknowledging that not everything in life is sunshine and rainbows. This chapter will explore 10 uncomfortable truths about life that might challenge your perceptions and force you to confront the hard realities. Often ignored or overlooked, these truths can provide valuable insights and inspire personal growth. So, let's dive in and explore these uncomfortable truths, accompanied by thought-provoking quotes from unknown sources.

1. A salary is the drug

In pursuing financial stability, we often compromise our dreams and passions. Our jobs become a comfortable routine, masking the burning desire for something greater. It's crucial to balance chasing our dreams and ensuring financial stability.

2. Don't waste your life waiting for the "perfect moment."

Delaying the pursuit of your goals in search of the perfect moment can lead to a trap. Life is unpredictable, and opportunities rarely come with perfect timing. Seize the moment, take risks, and make things happen rather than waiting for circumstances to align perfectly.

3. Even if you trust your most real friends and family, do not let them know anything about you

While trust is important, it's crucial to be discerning about the information we share. Not everyone deserves access to our innermost thoughts, dreams, and vulnerabilities. Guarding certain aspects of ourselves can protect us from unnecessary judgment or exploitation.

4. Start upgrading your life, and you'll lose 99% of your close friends

As we grow and evolve, our aspirations and priorities may change. Sometimes, personal growth leads us on paths that diverge from those of our friends. Embrace that not everyone will accompany you on your journey and focus on cultivating new relationships that align with your aspirations.

5. Government and politicians can never save you from your problems

It is crucial to acknowledge the constraints of political systems and the responsibilities of politicians in a realistic manner. While they can contribute to positive change, relying solely on them to solve our problems must be revised. It's crucial to take personal responsibility and work towards solutions ourselves.

6. Finding happiness can be enhanced by forgiving your parents and releasing them from blame for the challenges you face in life

Holding onto resentment and blaming our parents for our difficulties can hinder personal growth and happiness. Forgiving them doesn't mean forgetting or excusing past actions; rather, it allows us to free ourselves from anger and create a more positive future.

7. Develop the habit of intentionally allowing others to win arguments in order to safeguard your mental well-being

Not every battle is worth fighting, especially when it comes to maintaining our mental well-being. Sometimes, it's better to let others win arguments to prioritize harmony and peace over being "right."

8. **Maturity is cultivated by practicing the ability to not internalize or take things personally**

Taking things personally often leads to unnecessary pain and conflict. Learning to detach our self-worth from external events or opinions enables personal growth and emotional resilience.

9. **By age 30, your inner circle should focus more on making money, building your body, and starting a family**

While this statement may not apply universally, it highlights the importance of prioritizing personal growth and responsibility in early adulthood. Focusing on financial stability, physical well-being, and nurturing meaningful relationships can contribute to a more fulfilling life.

10. **Rather than relying on a multitude of self-help books, the key lies in taking action and cultivating self-discipline**

Self-help books can provide valuable insights but are only meaningful with action.

Words of Wisdom: Somebody is in the hospital right now begging God for the opportunity you have. Don't you dare go to bed depressed.

– Steve Harvey

Chapter 32

15 Unspoken Social Rules That Could Transform Your Life

Navigating social situations can often feel like a minefield, with unspoken rules and expectations that many of us intuitively follow. While these guidelines aren't always explicitly taught, adhering to them can significantly improve your relationships and social interactions. Here are 15 key social principles to keep in mind—small but powerful adjustments that can profoundly impact your personal and professional life.

1. Don't Call Repeatedly Unless It's Urgent

If someone doesn't pick up your call after two attempts, assume they are unavailable for the moment. They could be occupied, resting, or attending to something important. Repeated calls can come across as inconsiderate unless the situation is truly urgent.

2. Always Return Borrowed Money Without Prompting

If you borrow money from someone, make sure to return it promptly, even before they remind you. Failing to do so could strain the relationship and cause unnecessary awkwardness. By returning borrowed money on time, you show respect for the trust they placed in you.

3. Be Mindful of Expenses When Treated to a Meal

If someone invites you out and offers to cover the bill, it's best to refrain from choosing the priciest option on the menu. Being considerate of their generosity shows appreciation. In turn, make it a point to reciprocate the gesture by treating them to a meal the next time.

4. Treat Service Workers with Respect

Everyone deserves respect, regardless of their job title. Whether you're interacting with a waiter, cleaner, or driver, treat them with the same courtesy you'd extend to anyone in a position of authority. This not only reflects your character but also creates a more positive atmosphere for everyone involved.

5. Hold the Door for Others

If you're entering or exiting a building and notice someone approaching behind you, hold the door open for them. It's a small act of kindness that goes a long way, showing that you're considerate of others, regardless of their gender or social status.

6. Share Taxi Expenses Fairly

When sharing a taxi with a friend and they pay the fare, make sure to cover the cost the next time. This shows fairness and mutual respect in the relationship, preventing one person from feeling taken advantage of.

7. Respect Diverse Perspectives

When discussing opinions or engaging in debates, remember that others may have viewpoints that differ from your own. What seems right or obvious to you may look entirely different from their perspective. Recognizing and respecting these differences is key to healthy, constructive dialogue.

8. Avoid Interrupting Conversations

When someone is speaking, allow them to finish before jumping in with your thoughts. Interrupting can come off as rude and disrespectful, signaling that you're not truly listening. Allow others the opportunity to express themselves completely before offering your response.

9. Stop Teasing If It's Not Enjoyable

If you enjoy playful teasing but notice the other person doesn't seem to appreciate it, stop immediately. Teasing should never make someone uncomfortable. Pay attention to their reactions, and if they don't enjoy the banter, respect their boundaries and don't continue the behavior.

10. Always Say "Thank You"

Whether someone holds a door open for you, helps you with a task, or gives you a compliment, always express your gratitude. Saying "thank you" acknowledges their efforts and shows that you don't take their kindness for granted.

11. Don't Make Promises You Can't Keep

It's better to avoid making promises altogether than to break them. If you're unsure whether you can follow through on a commitment, be honest from the outset. Breaking promises can damage trust and credibility, so only make them when you're certain you can fulfill them.

12. Keep Secrets Confidential

When someone entrusts you with a secret, honor their trust by keeping it to yourself, no matter what happens in the future. Even if your relationship with that person changes, their confidence in you shouldn't be compromised. Respect their privacy and take their secret to your grave.

13. Respect Privacy When Viewing Photos

If someone hands you their phone to show you a picture, refrain from swiping through their gallery without permission. You never know what personal or sensitive content could be just a swipe away. Respect their boundaries by only viewing what they've shown you.

14. Be Punctual and Respect Others' Time

When you schedule a meeting with someone, prioritize arriving on time. Arriving late can signal that you don't value their time, which can be especially frustrating for those with busy schedules. Time management is crucial, and being prompt shows respect for others' commitments.

15. Be Mindful of Sensitive Topics in Conversations

It's important to be aware of your audience when discussing personal achievements or experiences. For instance, avoid discussing your financial success in front of someone struggling financially, or boasting about your family around someone who may be facing personal challenges. Sensitivity to others' situations can prevent hurt feelings and foster more empathetic communication.

Practical Tips for Implementing These Rules

- **Practice Active Listening:** Pay attention during conversations and avoid interrupting. Nod or use small affirmations to show that you're engaged.

- **Be Mindful of Time:** Always plan to arrive 10-15 minutes early to avoid being late for appointments. Time management apps or reminders can help you stay punctual.

- **Keep Communication Clear:** If you can't keep a promise, communicate that as early as possible. Being transparent is crucial for building and sustaining trust.

- **Show Appreciation:** Small gestures like sending a thank-you message after someone helps you can strengthen your relationship with that person.

- **Know When to Apologize:** If you accidentally break any of these social rules, acknowledge it with an apology.

Words of Wisdom: Miles to go before I sleep.

– Robert Frost

Chapter 33

Beware of The Paradox of Control

In our fast-paced, goal-driven world, the notion of control is often seen as the key to success and happiness. We strive to control our careers, relationships, finances, and even our emotions. The idea is that the more control we have over our lives, the more secure and content we will be. However, there exists a concept known as the "Paradox of Control," which suggests that the relentless pursuit of control can actually lead to increased stress, anxiety, and a diminished sense of well-being. Understanding this paradox is essential for achieving a balanced and fulfilling life.

The Illusion of Control

The Paradox of Control begins with the illusion that we can have complete control over every aspect of our lives. This belief is fueled by societal norms, self-help books, and motivational speakers who emphasize the importance of taking charge and being proactive. While there is some truth in the idea that taking responsibility for one's actions can lead to positive outcomes, it is unrealistic to believe that we can control everything.

Life is inherently unpredictable. External factors such as economic downturns, natural disasters, and health issues can disrupt even the best-laid plans. Additionally, other people's actions and decisions, which are beyond our control, can significantly impact our lives. The illusion of control can lead to frustration and disappointment when things do not go as planned, perpetuating a cycle of stress and anxiety.

a. The Stress of Perfectionism

One manifestation of the Paradox of Control is perfectionism. Perfectionists strive for flawless performance in all areas of life, believing that achieving perfection will grant them control over their outcomes. However, this mindset often backfires. The constant pressure to be perfect creates an environment of chronic stress and anxiety. Perfectionists become trapped in a cycle of never-ending self-criticism and fear of failure.

b. The Impact on Relationships

The Paradox of Control also extends to our relationships. Trying to control others, whether it's a partner, family member, or colleague, can lead to conflict and resentment. People resist being controlled and attempts to manipulate or micromanage them often backfire, resulting in strained relationships and increased stress.

c. Letting Go: The Path to True Freedom

The key to resolving the Paradox of Control lies in letting go. This does not imply surrendering accountability or turning inactive. Rather, it involves recognizing the limits of our control and focusing on what we can realistically influence. Letting go requires a shift in mindset, from trying to control everything to accepting uncertainty and embracing flexibility.

d. Focusing on What You Can Control

While we cannot control everything, we do have control over our actions, attitudes, and responses. By focusing on these aspects, we can navigate challenges more effectively. This approach empowers us to take proactive steps toward our goals without becoming overwhelmed by factors beyond our control.

e. Practicing Mindfulness

Mindfulness is a powerful tool for managing the Paradox of Control. By staying present and fully engaging with the current moment, we can reduce the tendency to ruminate on past events or worry about the future. Mindfulness helps us develop a sense of acceptance and equanimity, allowing us to respond to life's challenges with greater clarity and calmness.

f. Cultivating Acceptance

Acceptance is not about resignation or giving up. It is about acknowledging reality as it is and finding peace within it. Cultivating acceptance allows us to let go of the need for control and find contentment in the present moment. This shift in mindset can lead to greater emotional well-being and a more balanced approach to life.

The Benefits of Letting Go

Letting go of the need for control can have profound benefits for our mental and physical health, relationships, and overall quality of life. By embracing the Paradox of Control, we can:

i. **Reduce Stress and Anxiety:** Accepting uncertainty and focusing on what we can control helps alleviate the chronic stress and anxiety associated with trying to control everything.

ii. **Improve Relationships:** Letting go of the need to control others fosters trust, respect, and deeper connections in our relationships.

iii. **Enhance Resilience:** Embracing uncertainty and flexibility makes us more adaptable and resilient in the face of life's challenges.

iv. **Increase Happiness and Fulfillment:** By accepting reality and focusing on the present moment, we can find greater contentment and joy in our daily lives.

Words of Wisdom: You are totally replaceable at work. You're not replaceable at home. Home is your real life. Keep that perspective. Always.

– Shannon L. Alder

Chapter 34

Labor Omnia Vincit: Work Conquers All

Labor Omnia Vincit, a Latin phrase meaning "Work Conquers All," encapsulates a timeless belief in the power and significance of labor across cultures and throughout history. This motto serves as a poignant reminder of the transformative potential inherent in diligent effort and perseverance.

Meaning of Labor Omnia Vincit

At its core, Labor Omnia Vincit emphasizes the idea that through industrious work and dedication, individuals can overcome challenges, achieve success, and effect positive change in their lives and communities. The phrase underscores the inherent value of labor, not merely as a means of economic sustenance but also as a pathway to personal fulfillment and societal progress.

In contemporary contexts, Labor Omnia Vincit resonates deeply in various spheres, including business, education, and personal development. It encourages individuals to embrace hard work, resilience, and determination as essential virtues in the pursuit of their goals and aspirations.

Origin of Labor Omnia Vincit

The origin of Labor Omnia Vincit can be traced back to ancient Roman times, reflecting the ethos of Roman society where labor was highly regarded and considered integral to the prosperity of the state. The Romans, known for their engineering marvels, military prowess, and civic achievements, attributed much of their success to the diligent labor of their citizens.

The phrase is frequently connected with Virgil, one of Rome's earlier most famous writers. In his work "Georgics," Virgil extolled the virtues of agriculture and labor, emphasizing their vital role in sustaining civilization and ensuring its continuity. The famous line "Labor omnia vicit improbus" from the Georgics encapsulates this sentiment, with "improbus" conveying the idea of persistent or relentless labor.

Over time, Labor Omnia Vincit has transcended its origins in Roman literature to become a universal maxim, celebrated for its enduring relevance and inspirational value. It serves as a testament to the timeless nature of human endeavor and the indomitable spirit of those who embrace the challenges of work with dedication and purpose.

Contemporary Relevance

In the contemporary world, Labor Omnia Vincit continues to inspire individuals and communities facing diverse challenges. It resonates with professionals striving for excellence in their careers, entrepreneurs navigating the complexities of business, and students pursuing knowledge and skills to shape their futures.

Business leaders often invoke the spirit of Labor Omnia Vincit to foster a culture of hard work, innovation, and perseverance within their organizations. By encouraging employees to embody these values, companies can cultivate a productive workforce committed to achieving collective goals and driving sustainable growth.

Educators also uphold the principles of Labor Omnia Vincit in their efforts to empower students with the knowledge, skills, and work ethic necessary for success in an increasingly competitive world. By instilling a strong sense of purpose and resilience, educators prepare future generations to confront challenges with confidence and determination.

Embracing the Timeless Philosophy of "Work Conquers All"

Beyond its historical roots and contemporary applications, Labor Omnia Vincit resonates as a timeless philosophy that transcends cultural boundaries. It serves as a universal call to action, urging individuals to harness their skills and efforts towards constructive ends. Whether in the pursuit of personal goals, the advancement of professional endeavors, or the betterment of society as a whole, this motto embodies the enduring spirit of human achievement through diligent labor. By embracing the ethos of Labor Omnia Vincit, we affirm our commitment to perseverance, excellence, and the transformative power of work in shaping a brighter future for ourselves and generations to come.

Words of Wisdom: Greatness needs luck, but it's never by accident.

– Barack Obama

Chapter 35

The Empty Boat and Young Monk

A long time ago, a young Zen monk lived in a little monastery in the forest by a small lake. The monastery was occupied by a few older monks, but the remainder were beginners who still needed to learn. The monks had numerous tasks at the monastery, but one of the most essential was their daily routine, which required them to sit down, close their eyes, and meditate. The monk struggled to focus during his meditation practice for several reasons, which irritated him. After that, I concentrated in quiet for hours at a time. After each meditation, they were to report back to their mentor on their development.

Anger of a Young Monk

When the young monk reported his progress, or lack thereof, to his mentor, the senior monk asked him a simple question with a hidden lesson: "Do you know what is making you angry?"

The young monk responded, "Well, normally, as soon as I close my eyes and begin to meditate, someone moves around and I lose focus. I am angry when someone disturbs me even when they are aware that I am meditating. How couldn't they be more considerate? When I close my eyes again and try to focus, a cat or a tiny animal may pass by and distract me again.

At first glance, the object of the novice monk's anger seemed to be external – an arrogant fellow monk who constantly berated and belittled him. However, the master encouraged the novice to look deeper, beyond the apparent cause of his anger. In the stillness of the monastery, the master guided the young monk to introspect and inquire within.

I become upset even when the wind blows and the tree branches make noise. If it wasn't enough, the birds kept singing, and I couldn't seem to find rest in this area." The senior monk calmly stated to his student, "I observe that you get furious with each interruption you meet. This is the exact opposite of the goal of your meditation practice. You, whatever it is."

Should discover a technique to not become irritated with people, animals, or anything else around you that irritates you throughout your job. Following their discussion, the young monk left the monastery and searched for a calmer location where he could meditate undisturbed. He discovered such a location at the neighboring lake's beach. He brought his mat, sat down, and began to meditate.

But suddenly, a flock of birds splashed into the lake near where the monk was meditating. Hearing their ruckus, the monk opened his eyes to see what was happening. Although the lake's shore was calmer than the monastery, there were still things that disturbed his tranquility, and he became upset once more. Even though he couldn't find the tranquility he sought, he continued going to the lake. Then one day, the monk noticed a boat tethered to the end of a little pier. And then an idea struck him: "Why don't I take the boat, row it down to the center of the lake, and meditate there?

"Nevertheless, there isn't going to be anything to bother me I'm in the midst of the lake." He drove the boat to the middle of the pond and began to relax. As intended, there was nothing in the lake's core to disturb him, so he could concentrate all day. After the day, he returned to the monastery. This went on for a few days, and the monk was happy to have finally found a place to meditate in peace. He hadn't been annoyed, so he could continue his meditation practice peacefully.

On the third day, the monk sat in the boat, rowing to the center of the lake, and resumed his meditation. A few minutes later, he heard splashing water and felt the boat moving. He became agitated because someone or something was bothering him in the middle of the lake. When he opened his eyes, he saw a boat heading directly for him. He hollered, "Steer your boat away, or else you will hit my boat." However, the second boat continued to approach him, only a few feet away. He cried again, but nothing changed, and the oncoming boat struck the monk's boat. Now he was enraged.

He raised his voice, "Who are you, and why have you hit my boat in the middle of this vast lake." There was no response. This made the young monk even more furious. He rose to see who was in the other boat, but to his amazement, there was no one in it. The boat had presumably drifted along in the breeze and collided with the monk's boat.

The monk's rage subsided. It was only an empty boat! There was no one to be upset with. At that point, he recalled his mentors' query, "Do you know what is making you angry?" And then pondered, "Is it not other people, situations, or circumstances?" My fury stems from my reaction to the empty boat, rather than the boat itself. All of the individuals or events that irritate and anger me are like an empty boat. They can't make me mad unless I react." The monk rowed the boat back to shore. He returned to the monastery and began meditating with the other monks.

There were still noises and disruptions, but the monk dismissed them as an "empty boat" and proceeded to meditate calmly. When the senior monk noticed the change, he simply told the young monk, "I see that you have identified and overcome the source of your anger."

Words of Wisdom: If I am worth anything later, I am worth something now. For wheat is wheat, even if people think it is grass in the beginning.

– Johann Wolfgang von Goethe

Chapter 36

Nana Korobi, Ya Oki: Seven Falls, Eight Rises

In the journey of life, setbacks are inevitable. The phrase "Nana korobi, ya oki" in Japanese provides an essential message about tenacity in the midst of adversity. Translated as "Fall seven times, rise eight," this saying embodies the spirit of perseverance, determination, and the belief that every fall is an opportunity for even greater ascension.

Understanding the Proverb

"Nana korobi, ya oki" is based on the philosophy of Zen and shows an outlook that recognizes the inevitable nature of failure and the value of perseverance. It suggests that each time we fall (whether metaphorically or literally), we should not only get back up but also rise stronger and wiser than before. This mindset is crucial in navigating life's challenges, as it encourages a continuous cycle of learning, growth, and self-improvement.

The Symbolism of Seven Falls and Eight Rises

The specific numbers in the proverb carry symbolic meaning:

- Seven Falls: Represents the setbacks, failures, or challenges that one may encounter in life. It acknowledges that difficulties are part of the journey and cannot be avoided.

- Eight Rises: Signifies resilience and the ability to transcend those challenges. It implies that we should never be defeated by setbacks but instead use them as stepping stones to greater success.

This symbolism underscores a crucial aspect of personal development and resilience: the understanding that setbacks are not permanent obstacles but opportunities for growth and transformation.

Applying the Proverb in Real Life

1. **Personal Growth and Development**

   Setbacks frequently act as spurs for reflection and development in the process of personal growth. Each failure or setback presents an opportunity to learn from mistakes, reassess goals, and develop resilience. People who embrace the philosophy of "Nana korobi, ya oki" understand that setbacks are not indicative of failure but rather a natural part of the journey toward success.

2. **Professional Success**

   In the realm of career and professional life, setbacks such as job rejections, business failures, or setbacks in projects can be disheartening. However, those who embody the spirit of the proverb view these setbacks as chances to refine their skills, pivot their strategies, or even embark on entirely new paths. This resilience often distinguishes successful entrepreneurs, leaders, and professionals from those who are easily discouraged by challenges.

3. **Cultural and Historical Significance**

   The proverb "Nana korobi, ya oki" has deep cultural roots in Japan, where it is often used to inspire perseverance in the face of adversity. It has been passed down through generations as a reminder of the strength and resilience inherent in human nature. Beyond Japan, its wisdom resonates globally, transcending cultural boundaries to become a universal symbol of perseverance.

Philosophical Insights

1. **Zen Buddhism Influence**

   The influence of Zen Buddhism on the proverb is profound. Zen teachings encourage meditation, embracing fragility, and perseverance in the face of adversity. "Nana korobi, ya oki" aligns with these principles by encouraging individuals to accept setbacks without despair and to view them as opportunities for spiritual and personal growth.

2. **Resilience and Mental Health**

   From a psychological perspective, the ability to bounce back from setbacks is closely tied to mental health and well-being. Individuals who practice resilience techniques, such as reframing setbacks as learning experiences or maintaining a positive outlook, often exhibit greater emotional strength and adaptability in coping with stress and adversity.

Practical Applications

1. **Strategies for Building Resilience**

   - **Mindfulness and Self-awareness:** Cultivating mindfulness helps individuals stay present and grounded during challenging times.

   - **Adaptive Thinking:** Developing a growth mindset allows for flexible thinking and problem-solving in the face of setbacks.

   - **Seeking Support:** Building a strong support network provides emotional validation and practical assistance during difficult periods.

2. **Learning from Setbacks**

- **Reflection:** Spending time to think about failures can help people discover insights learned and opportunities for development.

- **Goal Setting:** Setting realistic goals based on newfound insights increases the likelihood of success in future endeavors.

Words of Wisdom: Sooner or later, those who win are those who think they can.

– Richard Bach

Chapter 37

Are you a time billionaire?

In the race of life, where success is often measured in achievements, wealth, and possessions, it's easy to overlook our most valuable asset: time. Graham Duncan's concept of the "Time Billionaire" challenges us to reconsider our perspective on life. While we idolize financial billionaires, few of us truly appreciate the wealth of time we possess, especially in our youth.

Are you a time billionaire?

Consider this: At the age of 20, you have approximately two billion seconds left, assuming an average lifespan of 80 years. This vast reservoir of time is a remarkable endowment, yet it's often squandered or taken for granted. We live in a world where the pursuit of money and material possessions overshadows the significance of time—an asset far more limited and irreplaceable than any other.

The Stoic philosopher Seneca, in his treatise "On the Shortness of Life," aptly points out that our lives are not inherently short; it is our misuse and squandering of time that makes them seem so fleeting. We are given an ample supply of time, yet we often fail to use it wisely. Being a "Time Billionaire" isn't about having an abundance of time, but rather recognizing and cherishing the finite moments we possess.

Tim Urban's ingenious "Life Calendar" visualizes this concept beautifully. Each square represents a week of your life, a stark reminder of time's passage and the diminishing resources at our disposal. As you fill in these boxes, it becomes evident how swiftly time elapses, urging us to make the most of every moment.

The birth of a child can profoundly shift our perspective on time. Suddenly, we are entrusted with a new life, and the awareness of time's preciousness intensifies. The encounter with the older man, reflecting on his daughter's swift journey into adulthood, serves as a poignant reminder of the fleeting nature of time.

It's easy to get caught in the trap of constantly striving for more—more success, more possessions, more experiences—without ever pausing to appreciate the present. We envision milestones that promise fulfillment: "I can't wait until I'm 18 so I can [X]." "I can't wait until I'm 25 so I can [Y]." "I can't wait until I'm 45 so I can [Z]." Yet, this mindset perpetuates a cycle of anticipation, where we chase after the next goal without ever relishing the present moment.

The epiphany of having "enough" is transformative. It's a realization that the pursuit of endless accumulation is futile if it detracts from life's inherent joys. Time, as the ultimate currency, demands our utmost respect and consideration. It's the thread that weaves our experiences together, defining the quality and depth of our existence.

In navigating this journey, there are no definitive answers—only reflections and insights to guide our perspective on time. It's about asking the right questions and fostering a mindset that values the present. Time cannot be hoarded or bought; it can only be spent. Therefore, it is imperative to invest it wisely—in moments of love, connection, and purpose.

As we ponder the notion of becoming "Time Billionaires," let us remember that our wealth lies not in the accumulation of hours, but in the intentional and mindful use of each passing second. Treat time as your most precious resource, and you will discover that true richness is found in the moments you create and cherish with those you hold dear.

Words of Wisdom: The world will ask who you are, and if you do not know, the world will tell you.

– Carl Jung

Chapter 38

8 Powerful Signs You're Thriving

In a world where it's easy to focus on what we lack or aspire to achieve, recognizing and appreciating the signs of thriving can be uplifting and grounding. Thriving isn't just about reaching lofty goals; it's about finding satisfaction and fulfillment in the everyday aspects of life. Here are eight powerful indicators that you are indeed thriving:

1. You Have a Safe Place to Call Home

A place where you feel secure and can retreat from the world is a fundamental sign of thriving. It means you have stability and a sanctuary to recharge. Your home represents a space where you can truly be yourself and create a sense of belonging. Whether it's a cozy apartment or a sprawling house, having a roof over your head symbolizes a stable foundation on which you can build and flourish.

2. You Harbor Genuine Wishes for Others

Thriving goes beyond self-contentment; it includes the ability to extend goodwill towards others. When you genuinely wish for the success and happiness of those around you, it reflects a positive mindset and a generous spirit. This empathy and compassion indicate that you are not only focused on your own needs but also care about the well-being of others, which enhances your own sense of fulfillment.

3. You Enjoy Fresh and Clean Clothing

The simple act of wearing clean clothes may seem trivial, but it's a sign of personal well-being and self-care. It indicates that you have the means to maintain personal hygiene and take care of your basic needs. Clean clothes are a reflection of your ability to manage everyday tasks and take pride in your appearance, contributing to a positive self-image and overall sense of thriving.

4. You Have a Supportive Presence in Your Life

Thriving often involves having someone who genuinely cares about you. Whether it's a friend, family member, or partner, having a supportive presence in your life provides emotional nourishment and encouragement. This connection not only helps you navigate life's challenges but also reinforces your sense of belonging and value, which is crucial for your overall well-being.

5. You Are Alive and Breathing

The very act of breathing signifies life and vitality. It may sound basic, but the simple fact that you are breathing and alive is a powerful reminder of your existence and potential. Each breath you take represents an opportunity to embrace life, pursue your passions, and make the most of the present moment. It's a fundamental sign that you are thriving in the most essential way.

6. You Have Access to Clean Water

Access to clean water is a vital aspect of thriving. It is essential for health, hydration, and daily functioning. When you have access to clean water, it reflects not only your basic survival needs being met but also your ability to maintain a healthy lifestyle. It underscores a level of comfort and security that supports your overall well-being.

7. You Possess a Kind and Compassionate Heart

A good heart is a hallmark of thriving. It means you approach life with kindness, empathy, and integrity. Having a compassionate heart enhances your relationships and interactions, fostering positive connections with others. It signifies that you are not only focusing on your own needs but also contributing positively to the world around you.

8. You Have Nourished Yourself Today

Eating food is more than just a necessity; it's a sign of self-care and sustainability. If you've eaten today, it indicates that you are meeting your basic nutritional needs and taking care of your body. It's a reflection of your ability to provide for yourself and ensure that your health and well-being are prioritized.

Words of Wisdom: Don't live the same year 75 times and call it a life.

– Robin Sharma

Embrace the Power of "Inverse Paranoid"

Inverse Paranoid explores wisdom, resilience, and personal growth, revealing life as a series of opportunities, even in challenges. Embracing simplicity and learning from adversity, transforms obstacles into stepping stones.

The philosophy of "Inverse Paranoid" invites us to believe that the universe conspires in our favor. Each setback holds a lesson, and each challenge is a hidden blessing. By adopting this perspective, we cultivate resilience, productivity, and clarity, empowering ourselves to live a life of purpose and fulfillment.

Remember, the true luxuries of life lie not in material abundance but in balanced living, meaningful connections, and the courage to embrace the unknown. Armed with the lessons and strategies in this book, you hold the tools to navigate life's complexities with confidence and grace. Let the principles of Inverse Paranoid guide you toward a future where challenges transform into triumphs, and life unfolds as a gift designed for your ultimate growth and happiness.